Back to Common Sense

Rethinking School Change

Joe Dawidziak

ROWMAN & LITTLEFIELD EDUCATION
A division of
ROWMAN & LITTLEFIELD PUBLISHERS, INC.
Lanham • New York • Toronto • Plymouth, UK

Published by Rowman & Littlefield Education
A division of Rowman & Littlefield Publishers, Inc.
A wholly owned subsidiary of The Rowman & Littlefield Publishing Group, Inc.
4501 Forbes Boulevard, Suite 200, Lanham, Maryland 20706
http://www.rowmaneducation.com

Estover Road, Plymouth PL6 7PY, United Kingdom

Copyright © 2010 by Joe Dawidziak

All rights reserved. No part of this book may be reproduced in any form or by any electronic or mechanical means, including information storage and retrieval systems, without written permission from the publisher, except by a reviewer who may quote passages in a review.

British Library Cataloguing in Publication Information Available

Library of Congress Cataloging-in-Publication Data
Dawidziak, Joe, 1972-
  Back to common sense : rethinking school change / Joe Dawidziak.
    p. cm.
  ISBN 978-1-60709-559-0 (cloth : alk. paper) — ISBN 978-1-60709-560-6 (pbk. : alk. paper) — ISBN 978-1-60709-561-3 (electronic)
  1. School improvement programs. 2. School management and organization. 3. Educational change. 4. Strategic planning. I. Title.
  LB2822.8.D38 2010
  371.2'07—dc22
                                                                    2010004770

$\circledcirc^{\text{TM}}$ The paper used in this publication meets the minimum requirements of American National Standard for Information Sciences—Permanence of Paper for Printed Library Materials, ANSI/NISO Z39.48-1992.

Printed in the United States of America

Contents

Introduction — 1

1. The Trap of Success — 9
2. It's Not Fair — 15
3. Getting the Right Fit — 23
4. The Train Is Leaving the Station — 41
5. Well, Well, Well — 49
6. Money Is the Answer—To Nothing — 59
7. Perception vs. Reality — 65
8. What Questions Do You Have? — 71
9. The One-Hundred-Yard Rule — 79
10. Long Division — 85
11. Let the Problem Ripen — 91
12. If It's Broke, Fix It with Duct Tape; If It's Not Broke, Break It, Then Fix It with Duct Tape — 97
13. Remembering Where You Came From — 103
14. The Final Story — 109

Conclusion 119

References 129

About the Author 131

Introduction

> Perhaps the sentiments contained in the following pages, are not yet sufficiently fashionable to procure them general favor; a long habit of not thinking a thing *wrong*, gives it a superficial feeling of being *right*. —Thomas Paine, *Common Sense*, 1776

A little while ago, in 1776, a man named Thomas Paine wrote a book called *Common Sense*. It was written in a time of great uncertainty during the infancy of this great nation. Many things hung in the balance and chaos reigned in many areas of society. Thomas Paine's famous work brought normalcy back to the everyday lives and, more importantly, into the minds of the men and women living and making important decisions for the country and for their families during that time.

With the rapidly changing times today, the recent state of the economy, and the initiatives coming fast and hard from all walks of life, a parallel can be made that education is much in the same state today as the country was back then. Professional leaders in education wonder where to turn for answers and how to combat the many issues and philosophies thrown at them from different directions. There is a simple answer and it is right under our noses and it is free. It's called common sense.

Like other texts, the layout of this book is designed with a purpose. Much like school change, it is ugly at the beginning but beautiful in the end. What that means is that the ugly, difficult topics are covered first in order to get to the good juicy stuff later. School change can be rough around the edges and extremely difficult and contentious in the beginning, especially if it is not initiated in the correct manner. Whether the transition to change was very rough or very smooth, if you can survive the initial implementation and the actual process that follows, the end can be a hugely successful and beautiful thing.

That's kind of how I feel about this book. As you read the text, the further along you get, hopefully the more frequently you have "aha" and "duh" moments. This will happen because everything written here is common sense and you will understand that more fully the further along you read.

There is significance to the cover of this book that I don't want to be missed. As we all know, there were some positive attributes to having a one-room schoolhouse that are missed in today's educational world. In our hurry to advance we have, to a small degree, forgotten that the teacher is really supposed to know the students. The parents are really supposed to know the teacher. Regardless of whether any of those parties liked each other, reason and common sense could easily be applied to the handling of situations and to the notion of school change. It was more common to think before you acted, and it was the expectation that students do the same.

The importance of and the ability to teach content come and go with societal changes, but there are some things that should remain constant—things like building character and teaching respect for what is right and wrong, how to follow through, the importance of caring about others, and perhaps, most of all, patience. Simple foundations in education have been lost in our race to advance test scores, create high stakes accountability, and satisfy political and business leaders. As we look at the cover photograph we see our lost foundations that have disappeared over the years. What happened?

As depicted on the cover, some school districts have become so far removed from the commonsense values and traditions of the days of the one-room schoolhouse that they are no longer able to retrieve them again. How sad. As much as our students have advanced with today's technological world, it is really the one-room schoolhouse commonsense guidance that they seek and that they need. Believe it or not, those students know that it is the commonsense values that guide decision making. And they know they need commonsense values to successfully apply the advanced skills that they possess to the world around them. When we lock them out of that world and when we lock our own eyes and minds from seeing what they see and from thinking how they think, school change in the classroom and in the district becomes next to impossible. Even when it does happen, it will not stand the test of time.

We have come a long way in education and I thank my lucky stars for that every day. With that being said, it is still important to reflect on the schools of yesterday, the leaders within their walls, and the philosophies they followed that are embedded in the history of education. They were the pioneers that helped us to get to where we are today in education. It was they who paved the way for successful school change. As far as we advance we still have much to learn from the one-room schoolhouse. It's time to get back to common sense when confronting school change.

A former principal and mentor used to tell me that common sense will always prevail. It is obviously not his original quote, but he had the weathered face and the checkered career of an expert in this field. "Remember," he would say, "even in a school's darkest hour, common sense will prevail." Every once in a while, this saying comes back to me when all seems lost, especially in education.

There are many books published, especially in recent years, trying to describe and prescribe ways a school district can successfully improve some area of education, increase test scores, and accomplish successful school change. Without listing all of those resources, it is safe to say that most professional leaders in education know that it has become easy to get caught up in all of the movements. Sometimes for good reason, it may be added, as those movements often have significant positive impact on education today.

For the purpose of this book, the term *professional leader* in education does not refer to administrators, as is the assumption of a lot of people both in and out of the profession. Any person who stands in front of a group of others is a professional leader. Professional leaders are school administrators, but they are also teachers; board members; paraprofessionals; office, lunch, and custodial staffs, and so on. The term professional leader is used throughout this book, and it is imperative the reader understand that the term professional leader is inclusive.

Many researchers, professional leaders, and experts in our field are knowledgeable about educational reform. I am not one of them. When I talk about getting "back to common sense," I'm not talking about some new-fangled approach to raising test scores, improving the collaboration process, developing your professional learning community, or building leadership capacity. Those things have been adequately covered in a variety of other works. They are all the possible results of following the simple advice offered here. That is the point or the message of this book. A commonsense approach to educational improvement, as opposed to concentrated effort on individual processes, is what can contribute to successful school transition and successful school change. Schools do a great job of concentrating all of their efforts on one improvement project, and then another, and then something new. A commonsense approach, focusing broadly on the many facets of high-quality schools, is a major factor in creating successful school change.

Using technology as both a model and motivator, an innovative principal once created a movie highlighting various aspects of the district. The message was really intended for professional leaders who had been there for more than five years and the message was very simple. It was intended to get professional leaders to think about some questions: For the rest of this school year, what will they see? What will their students see? In guiding professional leaders to think about the answers to those two questions, the movie ended by suggesting that the answers to those two questions would make professional leaders remember why they got into this game in the first place. By writing this book I too am hoping not only to remind you why you got into this game but to encourage you to think about how to act on it again as well.

While the principal's media technology took those staff members back to thinking about things using their own common sense, I am hoping to do the same here. Instead of worrying about who has the most prep time or whether or not they were going to be paid for volunteering on a committee, they began to think like they did when they first started teaching. They began asking the right questions like they did earlier in their careers: What is best for kids? What is best for the district? And once they began to ask those questions again, they remembered more and more of the answers. They remembered why they got into the game of education in the first place.

Like some others in education I have been guilty of losing my place. At certain times in my career, other things, usually because they were controversial, seemed to become more important than the reason I got into education. I lost focus of what is important. It is a mistake I am embarrassed to admit that I have made more than once.

I hope this is a mistake you have never made. If you are like me, however, keep in mind that you are lucky. Every day is a new day in education. It is the only professional field that I know of that is forgiving in that way. Even after making a mistake, you have the chance to change the course of history, to make a difference in a child's life, to change the world in your own little way. So when it comes to successful school change, whether you are a leader or a follower, remember that right is right no matter what or who gets in the way. If you can always keep what is best for students at the forefront of your mind, whether you are in the classroom or the office, the controversy of the change itself will fade away in time. It always does. If you can do that, the change you know is right for kids will stand the test of time, and so will you.

And though it was more than two hundred years ago, with the following passage, I believe Mr. Paine would have agreed:

> And however our eyes may be dazzled with snow, or our ears deceived by sound; however prejudice may warp our wills, or interest darken our understanding, the simple voice of nature and of reason will say, it is right. —Thomas Paine, *Common Sense*, 1776

Good common sense sometimes involves trying to find a balance between promoting change and being critical of new things while never going whole hog one way or the other. Sometimes it is a very fine line to walk between aggressiveness and resistance when it comes to school change. We must remember that the newest educational book that comes out promoting this idea or that approach isn't always best for your district. Districts are as unique and individual as the children that fill their classrooms. Just because something is considered "best practice" doesn't always make it best practice for your district. Best doesn't always mean best.

Every district has its own unique demographics and as a result should have its own unique solutions to problems. It is healthy to look at what other districts have done to be successful, but it can also be terminally poisonous to rely on what others have done as a solution for your school or district. This is especially true when it comes to educating children, the most important profession in the world today. Use common sense to do what is best for your district. In the end, as the old mentor used to say, it is always common sense that will prevail.

Before you read chapter 1, there are two things that are critical to explain in order for you to clearly understand the content and the purpose of this book. First, I am not an expert. For the initial draft of this book, I began to do a lot of research. I even went so far as to jot down notes and quotes I wanted to support or refute. I also began a bibliography that included all the works of leaders at the forefront of education today. This included well-known authors I'm sure that you already know.

During the revision process, I happened to attend a dissertation conference, and it was during that conference that I had an "aha" moment. I realized that if I truly write about things that should be common sense regarding change in education, I can only write from the heart. I have written what I believe while rarely using other works either to support mine or to disagree with others.

To be sure, there is a selfish aspect to this as well. The bulk of the work on this book took place at the same time I was working on the initial writing of my own doctoral dissertation. Anyone who has been through this process knows that you begin to have so much of the space in your head taken up by other works and what others think, that there is sometimes little room for your own thoughts. I had had enough of research and wanted to do something to get my own thoughts back in my own head again, and express them in a way that might be helpful to others. In a way that might make some sense, common sense—that is—to others.

It is tough to write a book and a dissertation at the same time. Research for one was enough. So that will explain why you will see a limited bibliography at the end of this book. You won't see a lot of references to other works. All of that was taken out in the second revision because I wanted to do my own thing, express my own thoughts, and let the critics take a crack at that. There are always exceptions and that remains true here as well.

I feel strongly enough about chapter 5 that I left all of the references in, so the limited bibliography is mostly inclusive of this chapter. I hope after reading chapter 5, you will agree that the content is important enough to warrant citing research. In addition to research from chapter 5, it is important that professional leaders read Gary Vaynerchuk's (2009) book *Crush It*. Vaynerchuk's book does not pertain to education specifically, but it is incredibly motivating if you are into his sort of message. What is mirrored in his book are many of the same commonsense, right-under-your-nose solutions that are free if you know where to look. There are many other concepts from his book that can and should be applied to education, but more on that later.

The second thing I want to be clear about is that while all of the examples used in the book are real, for most of the examples I used I changed the location of the district and/or the professionals involved. It is important to understand this because otherwise you may be under the false impression that I am a world traveler, that I am well connected and know a lot of really well-connected professionals, and that I am knowledgeable about all sorts of school districts across the country and their trials and tribulations.

None of this is true, though again, all of the examples used are real, which does warrant merit. On the flip side, it would be a mistake to assume that the stories used are from the districts I have worked in as that also is false. What is true and real is that the examples used here are from a variety of districts, large and small, metropolitan and rural. What is important to remember is that the location is of secondary importance; it is the message or the lesson conveyed in the examples that is of primary importance.

Now, before you begin, let me ask you a couple of real commonsense questions to get you thinking. In *Common Sense,* Thomas Paine wrote that "when men have departed from the right way, it is no wonder that they stumble and fall." Have you ever felt as if you've lost your way, like you are simply stumbling from one issue to the next, from one lesson to the next? Do you remember why you got into this game of education, however long ago that was? Think so? What was the reason then and why should it be any different now? Chapter 1 might help clarify.

CHAPTER 1

The Trap of Success

THE STORY

This first story isn't entertaining. It isn't motivating or touching, and it isn't intended to inspire awe. It is simple and to the point. Fifteen years ago a medium-sized school district had an excellent superintendent, an experienced principal, and a staff that was second to none. They had a plan and the technology to see it through. They experienced a high level of success and were seen for a few years as a progressive leader in the field. Surrounding districts wanted to know what they did and how they did it.

Mr. Grant worked as a teacher in this district, and he was presented with a challenge from his principal and superintendent to increase test scores with a pilot group of students. He was asked to use data, try innovative teaching methods, and use alternate means of motivation. Mr. Grant had a high degree of success with his students, helping to improve test scores dramatically.

After making a pitch to the school board, Mr. Grant, the principal, and the superintendent tried this new approach with a much larger group of students. They experienced the same degree of success. The following year they were able to use the same approach with the entire district. The results were astounding.

A couple more years went by and the superintendent left for a larger district, the principal started to focus on retirement, and the staff assumed they had reached a pinnacle in education. And they began to slowly commit the cardinal sin in education: The district became stagnant. The professional leaders became stagnant. Now they are seen as having a toxic environment that is incapable of change. Which begs the question, what happened? The answer is as simple as the story itself. It is the trap of success.

THE THEORY

The trap of success can be the biggest obstacle to successful change in public school districts. But what is it? How does it happen? A lot of professional leaders in education concern themselves with helping districts respond to failure. What can be more dangerous and have more damaging, long-lasting negative effects is ignoring successful school districts and the focus they should have on change and continued growth. In districts that have already experienced some success there is a potential for the most important changes in education, yet those districts do not always reach their potential. Here's why. It is not how a district responds to failure that determines continued and sustained success. Rather, it is how a district responds to already achieved success that determines continued and sustained success.

Generally speaking, there are two ways that public schools respond to success. The first, and hopefully the most common, is to focus on continued growth, which breeds change and which results in continued growth and ongoing success. However, there are districts that allow themselves and their employees to get comfortable after experiencing success. They become stagnant. They have reached a comfort level that is discussed at length again in chapter 13. They assume they have achieved all that they can. This stagnancy leads to a vicious cycle of failure and negativity that repeats itself over and over again. Over time the culture becomes tarnished until someone or something intervenes.

Mr. Grant's story is unfortunate in that his success was the pinnacle of his career. His school district fell into the same cycle described above, and it remained in that cycle until there was a monumental intervention. So much time had passed, however, from the success to the intervention, that the time in between was spent just simply getting by.

Sometimes it begins with celebration, not the cautious kind, but the kind where professionals are congratulated, usually by each other, but sometimes by outsiders or outside agencies. Mr. Grant was excited

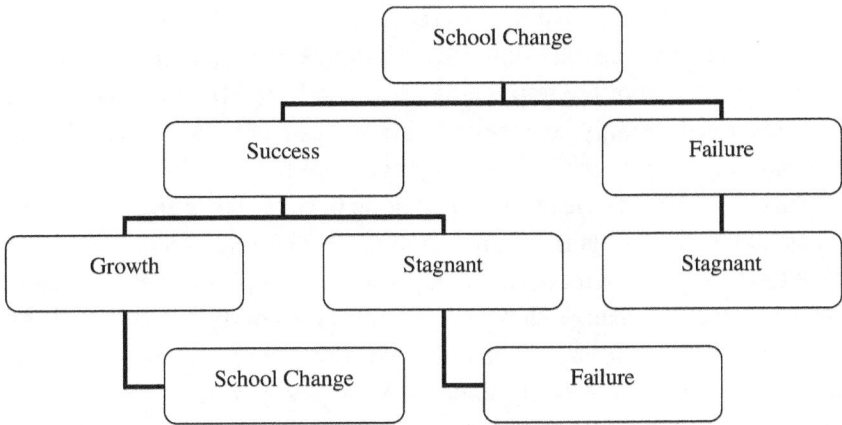

Figure 1.1. Chain of school growth or failure.

about the improving test scores in his school so he wanted to share the feeling of success with the rest of the faculty, staff, and students. In his district, the local newspaper provided coverage of how the school made such improvements. The media were asking questions in such a manner that school officials were placed in the role of all-knowing professionals.

Now they were being asked how to help the "other schools" who were still not raising test scores. The implication was that their problems were solved, so reminders of the work still to be done evaporated. With the congratulations, when there are no reminders of the work still to be done, there is no linkage of the success to a long-term strategic plan. And so the trap begins. Time passes and not only do they begin to think they don't have to change, they will encourage others to fight it. And revolting against change and the potential success and growth that comes with change will become the culture until someone or something breaks the chain (as seen in figure 1.1).

THE PRACTICE

The most dangerous thing about the trap of success is the inability of those going through the experience to recognize what is happening to them and to those around them. The failure to recognize events around them leads to professional leaders repeating negative behaviors without even recognizing they are doing so. I will talk more about this in a bit. The only way out of the trap is education itself. Whether in a successful district or a miserably performing one, the key is to be aware of your surroundings and to try to see things for what they really are.

This is sometimes easier said than done because there are a few more steps attached. Recognition isn't enough. Professional leaders must be able to recognize, then take advantage of small opportunities to pounce on a chance for change. If you have the rare ability to see things as they are, be the rare leader that also vocalizes what he or she sees. It means you have to tactfully express what you see happening to your surroundings, to those in it, and have suggestions to turn it around. It doesn't matter whether you are a teacher, an administrator, a school board member, or the lowest-ranking custodian in the building. Doing this will allow you to pounce on small opportunities for change. And the small ones always lead to the bigger ones. In fishing, they say where there are little fish, there are big fish, and that certainly applies when it comes to successful school change.

In the case of Mr. Grant's district, they used small fish to catch big fish and were able to temporarily create successful school change. However, the absence of the reminder of work still to be done, in this case, other ponds, lakes, and rivers to conquer, led to them standing and celebrating on the banks of a stagnant body of water that had no more fish left in it.

Earlier I mentioned that the failure to appropriately recognize one's surroundings leads to people repeating negative behaviors without knowing it unless someone or something points it out to them. I once sat in on a discussion by junior high teachers during a conference. All of them were concerned that the amount of detentions they were giving were not having an effect. In fact, many students turned it into a contest to see how many detentions they could get in a week. That's my kind of student, but that is a story for another book. The teachers' solution to this was to give more detentions. Baffling.

So I interrupted the discussion and put all of the teachers present in a scenario of my own. I asked them all to think about their own hypothetical sixteen-year-old teenagers driving around in their own cars that their parents had just bought for them. As the parent, you find out that the brakes in the car do not work. What do you do? Would you ask your child to keep driving around without brakes? Would you ask your own child to make a game out of trying *not* to hit anything, or do you go and get the brakes fixed? Think as if it was your own kid and you already know what the commonsense answer is.

We then talked about all of the other things that could be done instead of giving detentions. Later, I was talking with the group of administrators who were the direct supervisors. Some seemed to know the same thing that I did, but some did not. None of them, however, were able to express what needed to be expressed. I was lucky because I was an outsider. When I talked about the brakes in the car, they had an "aha" moment. And as obvious as it was to me, it was also equally as obvious that some of them had been caught in the trap of success. And a few of those professional leaders had been caught for such a long time that the damage may be irreversible. When I think about all of the students that have come before them and will continue to do so, it makes me wonder if those students get caught in the same trap that their teachers are in. And if so, that's just not fair.

CHAPTER 2

It's Not Fair

THE STORY

A group of undergraduate students were fortunate to have a teaching methods course with a revered professor named Pat Magestro. She repeated the same story to the class several times during the semester. The purpose of the repetition of the story was to drive home a point. The professor herself first heard the story told from Madeline Hunter. Those whippersnappers just entering the field probably have no idea who Madeline Hunter is, but those of us dinosaurs that have been around awhile know very well that she is a master of lesson planning and a legend in education. Anyway, the story first came up during a class discussion about what was fair and what was not fair. "Here's what you do when you become a teacher," Pat would say.

First, you take your class into the gymnasium. You line them up on one side of the gym and you ask them this question: "I want you all to run to the other end of the gym and back. Do you think you all can do that?" The answer, of course, is "Yes." "Okay, go ahead." When the class returns, ask the second question: "Now I want all of you to run to the other side of the gym and back and I want all of you to give me 100 percent effort. Do you think you can do that as well?" The answer again, of course, is "Yes." When the students return, ask them one final question. "Now I want all of you to run to the other end of the gym and back, give me 100 percent effort, and I want all of you to get back here at exactly the same time. Do you think you all can do that?"

Puzzled looks begin to appear on their faces. "That's not possible," Johnny states. "Why not?" the teacher asks. "Because Jerome is faster than I am," Sally states, putting her own two cents in. "Yeah, and Alicia is bigger than I am," another student adds. Soon the rest of the class begins chiming in with "Ladonis has longer legs than I do" and "I'm not that athletic" and "She's in better shape than I am."

"All of you are correct," the teacher explains. "It's not fair of me to ask you to do that, is it? It's not fair because you all run at a different pace. And you all run at a different pace for different reasons. Learning is a lot like that also. All of us learn at a different pace. Which means that you as a student will never be able to say to me as the teacher, 'That's not fair.'

"As the teacher, if I ask Jerome to do twenty questions and I ask Alicia to do ten questions, Jerome will never be able to say to me, 'That's not fair.' Because you all learn at a different pace, I as the teacher get to determine what is and what is not fair for each and every one of you separately. And Jerome, I will discuss your situation with you, but I will not discuss Alicia's situation with you. So you may not ask, 'Why do I have to do twenty questions, when Alicia only has ten?' I will discuss with you why you have twenty questions, but I will not discuss with you why Alicia only has ten.

THE THEORY

For the whippersnappers, I hope you were paying close attention. For the dinosaurs, maybe this story will make you smile a bit. Either way, imagine the power this story could have if applied to adults, and especially those of us in the field of education. We would simply do the job we were supposed to do without worrying about all of the other things going on around us. No jealousy, no feeling left out or underappreciated. We would be left with just a faithful commitment in ourselves and in our own ability to get the job done and to do it right.

Gaining the understanding that you as an individual do not have control over what is fair and unfair is an important first step in successful school change. As an individual professional educator, you do not have that control and yet if you understand that notion, you *do* have control over how that affects the quality of the work that you do. That, in turn, means that you unintentionally also have an effect on the quality of the work being done by the colleagues or students around you. There is a saying that applies here. Let your actions do the talking for you. You lead not with words, but by example. Right now a really good commonsense question you might be asking yourself is "How is it possible this is being written about? Isn't this just common sense?" You'd like to think so, but unfortunately, as I'm sure you've heard by now, common sense isn't always common.

When professional leaders want to implement school change, it has to start somewhere. I happen to think it begins with understanding the theory of the trap of success and then understanding the concept of what is fair and not fair. From there, if you are a teacher, everything associated with successful school change begins with the expert, and that typically means you. No matter how good an administrator may be, they are only as good as the teachers working for them.

That means that school change can only start with professional leaders that understand the concept of fair. It is those professionals that can drive an entire staff. They can drive the rest of the staff straight into the ground or wherever the district wants to go. Because if they understand the concept of fair as being out of their control, they can focus on helping the district in moving forward, as opposed to arguing, "This is not fair." They do the job they were hired to do, letting their actions speak for them, regardless of the change being asked of them. This is sometimes a rare combination of talent and character traits for a professional leader to possess.

As in Madeline Hunter's story, those professionals who "get it" will understand that it is up to some other higher person or some other higher group or thing to determine what is fair. And even though administrators and school boards are only as good as those below them, they are usually the ones making the call for the greater good of the district. Professional leaders who truly know this and accept this as professionals will realize that the higher-ups or the higher groups in education have the same interest that they do when trying to implement school change: we do what is best for kids and for the district. Period. It should always be about something bigger than all of us and not about what is best or "fair" for individuals.

All of us in education, at some point in time or another, have thought that something was unfair. Maybe someone across the hall has more prep time. Maybe your boss has allowed another coworker to spend more money on materials for the upcoming school year. Maybe you don't like the class you were given this year. Maybe you think the administration or the school board does not understand or appreciate what you do. Okay, this last part may actually be true in a lot of cases. With one or all of these situations, you may be right. But do not let that affect your professionalism and how you go about your own work.

Regardless of our roles in education, we like to consider ourselves as professional leaders and we like to think we act like professionals accordingly. Knowing this and taking into consideration what professional behavior should look like, rarely is it our place to deem what is fair or unfair. Rarely do any of us ever have all of the information necessary to make that judgment. There are two choices to be presented here. One is to say, "It's out of my hands," and not question what is happening or trust that those in charge know best. Or the solution could be to gain the information needed to make sound judgments and really change things.

We like to think in education that constant and extensive questioning should take place for good progress to occur naturally. Though this is certainly true, what we sometimes forget in this equation is that it is also sometimes okay to have some trust—not blind faith, but trust—in that the proposed change might be what is best for our students or for our districts, even if we can't see it right away.

In our behavior as professional educators and as school leaders, we should use common sense to deal with situations that aren't fair, whether they be inherited or created on the fly. We must understand that if we are the creator or a part of the situation, we take responsibility, correct our behavior and become a part of the solution accordingly, and move on. If we inherit the unfair situation, having the understanding that we may not have control over the situation allows us to behave and work appropriately and accordingly. And it is in our students' best interests to move forward while not worrying about the things we cannot control.

Common sense should tell us that what we can control is our response and our behavior and our work as professionals. Our appropriate behavior in turn models for our colleagues and for our students the appropriate behaviors necessary to promote change in a changing school environment. It also allows successful school leaders the continued ability to introduce and implement successful long-term school change that serves the interests of students, not the interests of what is or isn't fair. And if you can let your actions speak for you as a professional, those people that really matter will take notice.

THE PRACTICE

All action and effort in education should have purposeful meaning. What becomes difficult at times in education is trying to differentiate between what is worth putting that amount of effort into and what is not. Whether a teacher or an administrator, how do you tell if your action will produce results, or if the effort is worth it? When might you just be spinning your wheels and going through the motions?

Let's deal with these two questions separately. The first is more difficult. Sometimes you may never know there are results even though they exist. This is a common occurrence in our field. This frustrating experience may lead you to believe you are just going through the motions, but do not be deceived. If you are a teacher, you probably already know that most of the students whose lives have truly been changed because of your ability will never come back and thank you. Unless they go on to become famous, it is very likely you will never know what became of most of your students. The same is true for an administrator who has had a profound effect on a teacher, whether in the classroom or as a person. Even as adults, it is difficult to express gratitude appropriately. So sometimes when you don't see immediate results, you have to trust in yourself that you have done your job and done it well. And maybe more importantly, you may have to begin to trust that those around you have done the same.

On a smaller scale and as we all know, the knowledge that your action has purposeful meaning should have some direct or indirect correlation to students. Direct correlation means that a student understands something immediately as a result of some teaching methodology you successfully used. You can tell it, you can see it, and there is an immediate reward for both the teacher and the student. Indirect correlation means that maybe by participating in a district initiative to improve test scores you sit on a planning committee. You may not see the results of your input immediately or at all, but there is still an indirect correlation to students through the action you participate in. This you will likely never see, hear about, or be rewarded for.

The second question of when you might be spinning your wheels and going through the motions is a much easier one to answer. A very common characteristic that we all possess in education is a gut instinct that is usually pretty accurate. When you search deep down inside you, you know when you are not doing the best that you can. We all know when we haven't committed as fully as we should have. No one in education needs a book or a college professor to tell them that. Deep down, we know. Common sense alone should tell you to trust your gut instinct and let common sense prevail. The focus then should come in making that acknowledgment and making some changes. Be honest and fix it just like we would ask our students to do.

Everyone also knows that in education when you get hired, whether as an initial educator or a seasoned professional, you may get put into situations you didn't expect. Maybe you weren't told all of the information. Maybe you didn't ask either because you didn't think of it or you didn't want to know. Maybe you just didn't care. More than likely the latter is true because at the time you just wanted the job. Regardless, it may not always be the perfect situation that you thought it was when you arrived.

For others a bad situation may have manifested itself over the course of time. In all of these examples it would be easy for all of us at times to place blame. What is common among the administrative ranks is to place the blame on the predecessor. Using the story that she told as a springboard, Pat Magestro, the revered undergraduate professor, would certainly argue that placing blame is unacceptable professional behavior and most in our field would agree. But it happens all the time anyway. Even those that we think should know better do it sometimes. But regardless of how bad you think you may have it, no matter how much of a jerk your boss may be, we all knew to some degree what we were getting ourselves into. If you did not you were probably either incredibly naïve or you really didn't want to know. That much is common sense.

Not only is it sometimes healthy that unfair or bad situations should happen to all of us from time to time, an explanation is warranted as to why it is a necessary evil in the education profession. Bad situations and unfair events keep us all on our toes. Just the potential of a negative situation keeps educators in a consistent state of razor sharp and heightened awareness. Or it just keeps them really stressed out as discussed further in chapter 5. Either way, this is arguably one of the most positive attributes in a potentially negative situation to possess in the field of education.

Unfair situations are the perfect opportunity for professionals to create their own integrity. Easy for me to say I know. But really it is a chance to beat the odds. It is a rare opportunity to look adversity in the face hard and prove the rest of the world wrong. If you've been a subpar teacher or administrator, it is a true chance at redemption and to show that you can be great. If you are a very good teacher or administrator, it is another chance to confirm what those around you already know: that you are great.

If all else here fails and you just cannot get over the feeling that something is unfair, there is always option number two and it's discussed further in chapter 3. Get the right fit. If that means you are a teacher in the wrong place or an administrator with a teacher in the wrong place, get the right fit. Move on. Moving on does not mean you've failed. We all have choices in life; why not make the ones that not only make you happy, but can help kids in the long run? So if the idea of something or someone being unfair is getting in the way of school change and if change cannot happen with you, then let it happen without you.

CHAPTER 3

Getting the Right Fit

THE STORY

One fine spring day a potential teaching candidate was interviewing for a particular teaching job. Interestingly, the bulk of that interview was done one on one with the candidate and the principal of the school alone in an office. Not the way it is recommended by some to do it these days. Toward the end of the interview, the principal asked the candidate several questions about the future and how the candidate thought he fit into that particular district's future. The candidate's response to one of the questions was "In ten years I see myself sitting in that chair asking someone else the same question." That answer nearly left the principal speechless, though he was a veteran of twenty-five years at the time. He thought he had seen and heard it all. The candidate got the job and ten years later was proud to be asking other potential teaching candidates the same type of questions that his own principal had asked him all those years before.

THE THEORY

First of all, if you are a successful, established professional classroom leader, this might be the one chapter you might want to skip. If you are interested in how things could be done with cleaning the educational kitchen, determining tenure, and hiring, please read on. Secondly, everything about to be discussed here also *includes* administrators, a point not to be missed simply because the language used lends itself to the subject of teachers.

Successful change in schools and in education in general hinges almost entirely on the people you have in place. This shouldn't be a surprise to anyone. Much research has been done in this area to prove the concept to be true. This research includes all sorts of ideas about hiring the right people, properly professionally developing the ones you have, and weeding out those that really need to go.

Much research has also been done in the area of hiring and its process. Almost all relevant research in this area also concludes that having good professional leadership, whether in administration or in teaching, has the most direct and profound effect on student achievement. It makes sense that leadership ability or the capacity a candidate may have to develop leadership ability should be something that a school district should view as a priority in the hiring process. But before we can talk about the hiring process, we must first take a look at the cleaning process.

Though I'm not very good at it, I like to cook. For me, I like to make sure the kitchen is clean before I cook. This analogy could be applied to education. Make sure we remove the dirty things before we teach children. I'm not talking about the things you see on television or read in the paper. I'm talking about the less than 1 percent of professional leaders that are not interested in bringing their "A" game every single day they are in contact with students. You probably don't have any of these in your school, but if you do, get cleaning.

Like most cleaning, cleaning the kitchen is not fun. It is a lot of work when you know it might just get dirty again. Ridding a school of subpar professional leaders is not fun, it's not easy, and in a lot of cases, it's damn near impossible. However, as you are a true professional leader, it is a responsibility that you are obligated to perform regardless of its ugliness. Think about it on these terms. Would you really want your own children eating off of dirty dishes when it isn't necessary? Then think of the children in your building as your own.

On a side note, sometimes while I'm cleaning I get distracted and end up cleaning the cabinets, too, just for good measure. While you're replacing poor professional leaders with good ones or old professional leaders (really good, just retiring) with new ones, remember when you are implementing school change to follow the same procedure. Eliminate the old initiatives before instituting the new ones. Lay the groundwork for that first, but more on that later. For now, while you're already cleaning the kitchen, you might as well clean the cabinets too.

That means making an effort to find the initiatives that are outdated, not working, or too cumbersome. Get rid of the ineffective initiatives to make room for the new stuff. A professional leader from Detroit asked me how you can tell if they are effective or not. The easy answer is determining if the initiative is having any effect on student achievement. If so, is the effect happening at the pace it was intended? These are good rules of thumb.

All right, everything in the kitchen is clean, or at least as clean as it's going to get for now. Let's talk about the cooking. The key is finding the right ingredients. There are three elements that are critical in finding the right ingredients for successful long-term school change:

1. Creating a cleaning process: Devise a systematic approach for how your district will clean the kitchen.
2. Hiring: Revise your hiring practice and the hiring process.
3. Answering the question: To tenure or not to tenure?: Examine the district process/policy to determine whether or not to retain teachers for tenure.

So far this area has been covered in laissez-faire fashion. Now it is time to get a bit more serious. The second critical element in getting the right fit is the hiring and interviewing process for new teachers. Among many, many others, Douglas Reeves (*Leading Change in Your School*, 2009) has outstanding advice regarding proven interviewing techniques. They range from having candidates assess student data to evaluating student work. There are additions to be made to that advice. They include making the connection between a candidate's ability to assess and evaluate and real teaching competency. It also involves the realization that interviewing skills sometimes may have nothing to do with teaching ability. What Reeves's work also does not cover is the interview process itself. And it is in this area where the theory here really distinguishes itself in the "Practice" section later on.

The theory to begin with is very simple. Always hire professional leaders that are more educated, more knowledgeable, more talented, and that have more savvy than you do. The hiring process and some good rules of thumb will be covered extensively in the "Practice" section of this chapter, but just keep in mind that if there is an issue with a candidate after being hired and if all else fails in this area, see element number three.

Here's what common sense should tell you. If you get a gut feeling during an interview that the candidate may have what we will call "side issues," it may sometimes be okay to make a judgment call in the candidate's favor at that time, especially if you are in a pinch. However, in the first year after that particular candidate is hired, if you still have that gut feeling or if a new one arises, never take a chance. Do not renew that person's contract at the end of the first year. Cut your losses, in other words. It sounds cruel and harsh, but your students deserve the best.

A principal in a neighboring district expressed her frustration with a newly hired teacher. During the interview, the teacher expressed a desire and a willingness to coach, to volunteer for committees, and to chaperone dances. During the first year after being hired, the teacher did not follow through on any of those things. To make matters worse, the teacher also appeared to be a teacher only interested in coming in to work at 8:00 and leaving at 4:00, taking nothing home. What should the principal do? The teacher might turn into an excellent teacher. Unfortunately, there is only one thing to do: cut your losses. Do not renew.

A district should never take a chance on someone in that situation and here's the reason why. You must ask yourselves the following question: Are you really willing to potentially subject the students of your school to mediocre teaching for the next thirty years? Even if you are a teaching professional leader that hates your boss, you don't want your administrator or your school board answering yes to that question. Very few quality professional educators have said "yes" to that question and those that have should reevaluate their careers in education. School districts should begin to develop the philosophy that you only take the time, money, resources, and effort to professionally develop a sure thing. We owe that to our students and to our communities who are paying for our schools. That much is common sense.

A final point on this topic before moving on. Once in a while a top notch candidate came my way that I knew would only be around for a year or two because they were just that good. They'd be using our district as a stepping stone. Maybe they would end up moving on to a more lucrative district, maybe they would be moving up the ladder to administration, or maybe something more personal like having a baby and wanting to stay home. Regardless, when explaining the situation to my superiors, inevitably the question boiled down to: Do we really want to hire this person if they are only going to be around for a year or two?

If you are a true professional leader, the answer shouldn't even be a doubt in your mind. If you ever find yourself doubting yourself on this question, then be sure to remember to also ask yourself this one: Would you rather subject your students to the very best of professional leadership for a year or two, or would you rather pass up on a sure thing to hire an unknown and potentially subject your students or staff to mediocrity? If there is still a doubt left after answering this question, then you should probably absolve yourself altogether from the hiring process in your district.

The third critical element involves the determination of tenure. This element has the potential to be the most crucial in getting the right fit. It is the one and only easy chance for districts to correct any hiring mistakes. What some districts have run into multiple times either during the hiring process or shortly thereafter are outstanding candidates who possess what I have previously called "side issues." This poses several questions revolving around the balance of educational nature.

At what point do you determine that spending time and money on the professional development of a professional leader is not worth the effort due to the amount of time and energy spent helping the staff member work out his or her "side issues"? At what point do you come to the realization that all of the time and money spent on trying to professionally develop a staff member to the top of his or her game will never happen because that person has already hit the ceiling? Again, it sounds cold and brutally honest, but we owe it to our students to ask ourselves these questions.

In making determinations about investing time and energy into a professional leader to have the investment pay off for the district in the long-term future, I have developed what I call the plateau theory. Like everything you will read here, it is simple. As professional leaders we hope that all of our other professional leaders reach a plateau. The question is where is the plateau on the mountain? Is it halfway up or is it at the top? If they are only halfway up, do they have the fortitude to make the effort to reach the top? In case you haven't already figured it out, let me tell you, if the plateau is only halfway up the mountain, and that is as far as the professional leader can ever go, then Houston, we've got a problem.

A high school geography teacher (no pun intended here) struggled with classroom management. In the field of education, how you carry yourself is half the battle when it comes to classroom management. The other half is learning tricks of the trade. If you don't have experience, you can take classes and go to conferences to learn the tricks. At the end of the day, however, the tricks only get you halfway up the mountain and you plateau right there if you do not possess the right demeanor. This geography teacher took all the right classes, talked to the right people, and went to the right conferences to learn the tricks. She could talk the talk. However, she just didn't possess the right character traits to walk the walk. As a result, she will never plateau at the top of the mountain.

Cleaning the kitchen and determining tenure usually are the most uncomfortable things to deal with in the larger getting-the-right-fit process. In education, because of issues like tenure, the whole idea of incompetence can be a very controversial and difficult prospect. Through documentation, union red tape, and attrition through retirement, this process in reality could take years. Common sense tells us that it will be well worth the effort when considering strategic long-term planning for our districts, and we owe it to our students to follow through. On a positive note, we are talking about less than 1 percent of the professional leadership population and as a result, hopefully most of you will never have to deal with it at all.

In considering whether there is worth in the effort to rid the district of poor professional leaders, which as a reminder, *includes* administrators, the question that should be asked is: Are they part of the solution or part of the problem? The question itself seems simple. When broken down further, however, the question begins to become much more complex and the answer you thought was so clear may not necessarily be so.

The first part of the question deals with solution. Can this person be a part of a long-term solution? Though they may be subpar now, is there a chance they can contribute, even in a nontraditional or an unpopular way, to the success of the district over the course of time? If the answer is "yes," then they are a "keeper." Are they a part of the solution now but will be an impediment beyond this point in time? If the answer to this question is "yes," then you had better start the documentation and the kitchen cleaning process.

What muddies the water here is that sometimes we think people are a part of the problem when they may actually be a part of the solution. Yes, if you are willing to look at them objectively from a different point view, they are probably part of the solution. And in considering that point, now we could be talking about the students in your class as well.

Now that I've got you thinking about kitchen cleaning and tenure and how they can be either started or in the process, let's move on. It is uncomfortable and hard. It is time to change the subject and talk about something that should be beautiful and fun. I mean that and I am talking about getting the right fit through the hiring process.

THE PRACTICE

Earlier in this chapter I made a reference to the practice of hiring professional leaders that were better and more talented than you are. There are roadblocks to doing so. These employees that you hire and that are so wonderfully qualified may also show you up during a staff meeting from time to time. We are talking about teachers that some others may view as problems. They may be very high maintenance. They may be your biggest naysayers and biggest gossipers at times. But at the end of the day, they will also be your biggest supporters and most outspoken defenders in times of need if you have followed the change process carefully.

If you are a teacher reading this and you really think about it, the previous paragraph also applies to the students you teach. The biggest pains in the neck are sometimes your biggest supporters later in life when they have their own children. This will happen if you have done the process justice, believe me. The biggest smart alecks will go on in life and tell everyone they know how great you were. You'll find out why and how later in this book. For now, back to those high talented professional leaders that have been hired and that may also be a pain in the neck sometimes.

When they retire at the peak of their careers, at the top of their game, and after you may be long gone, those that will follow in your footsteps will wonder, Who was the person with the foresight to have put together such a dream team of professional leaders? And when these dream team professional leaders leave the profession it will create a vacuum in the district that will be impossible to fill. Others then will wonder, How did the person who hired them do it? They will want to research and repeat whatever process was used to get them in the first place. It is here in the practice that we will find the answers.

The best advice I could give to a school board is as follows: if you've hired quality professionals and you trust them (more on this later), then allow those you've hired to do their jobs. Allow the principal to do all of the interviewing for the school one on one with the teaching candidates. Allow the superintendent to do all of the interviewing one on one with principal candidates.

A quality administrator, superintendent, or principal needs to be trusted and counted on to do his or her job. And one of the most important parts of that person's job that should have been looked into when they were hired is being a phenomenal judge of pure professional leadership talent and making recommendations to the superintendent or the board or both. If you have a quality administrator, this is a skill that can easily be learned. The principal is typically the one and the only person who truly knows exactly what kind of a professional leader and what kind of a person will be just the right fit for whatever the position it is that is being hired for. Notice that I didn't say the best professional leader for the job. I said the best professional leader *and* the best person for the job.

Typically school districts on various levels want all sorts of people to be involved in the educational process to the highest degree. That is the "in" thing to do now. Scores of respected authors have used research to prove this inclusive process to be effective. And it is. However, the need for the degree of involvement called for by experts in the hiring process of a public school employee is arguable at best, in my opinion.

Here is where an old one-room schoolhouse method might be more effective than what some districts use today. There is a lot of room in the field of education for involvement and for input into the improvement of its processes. The hiring process isn't one of them. There is a very commonsense reason for this. You can learn about candidates as professional leaders no matter what process you use or how many people are involved in the process. The issue here is that you cannot get to know a candidate as a *person* using that type of intense involvement. Remember, you are looking for the best professional leader and the best person for the job all at the same time.

So you've posted the position and candidates are sending in their materials. What do you look for before the interview process? First of all, when you are posting the position, ask potential candidates to send five things in a specific order: a letter of interest, a resume, three letters of recommendation, a copy of transcripts, and a copy of licensure. The sequence you request doesn't have to be in this exact order; it is just a suggestion of what might be the most helpful. The idea is to see if candidates can follow directions. If two hundred candidates apply for one job, there must be a systematic way to weed them down to six to ten for interviews. There are several ways to do this, but only one that I prefer and that I think is more successful than the others.

The first screening is easy, but takes some work and should only be done by one person, which is usually the principal, to prevent variances in opinion from getting in the way. Create three piles. A "no" pile, a "maybe" pile, and a "yes" pile. The "no" pile is first in the sequence because this will be the largest pile. Any candidate that did not put the documents requested in the order requested will go in the "no" pile. No matter how good they may be, if they have followed instructions improperly, there is a chance they will continue to follow directions incorrectly after they've been hired. They go in the "no" pile.

After that, the second thing the screener will read is the letter of interest. Any spelling errors or grammatical errors will land a candidate in the "no" pile. Also added to that pile are credentials sent to the wrong person, the wrong school, and so on. Many times candidates are sending multiple application materials at a time using form letters and the like. As a result, many are not careful about remembering to change names, names of schools, and so forth. Again, if they are not careful and pay attention to detail here, they will not do so after they are hired. They go in the "no" pile.

A former student of mine applied for a teaching job. She spelled my name wrong and so I put her in the "no" pile. A while later she called to ask if I had received her materials. When I told her I had, she politely inquired as to why she was not considered. When I told her the reason why, she was embarrassed and apologized. She then asked if she would still be considered if she ever applied again. I assured her that she would be. A month later she applied for a different position. After spelling my name correctly the second time around, I realized in looking at her paperwork that she was an exceptional candidate. Our district would have really suffered without her. As it turned out she was hired and has proven an incredible talent as a professional leader.

In the content of the letter of interest, look for a few key words or phrases. "I have the ability to become an outstanding teacher" shows either a lack of competency now or a lack of confidence. Neither way you interpret that message is a positive sign. If there is not some phrase placing emphasis on caring for kids, they are a definite "no." A line about caring about kids or enjoying working with kids is an essential element that should be required. If the candidate writes a lot about experience as opposed to the quality of the experiences or if they write about things they have done instead of philosophy, they go in the "no" pile. Screeners should find things about experience and what they've done in the resume, not in the letter.

Here is a final addition about potential candidates' letters of interest. Public school districts generally shy away from letters with religious overtones. This is for good reason, which includes the First Amendment of the Constitution relating to the separation of church and state. If a candidate cannot realize that religious overtones in a letter of interest raise concerns, there is a strong chance they will not able to separate the two at some point in their teaching career. Keep in mind that this is not a slap in the face of any person who practices religion, but rather common sense in the field of public education. A letter of interest to a public school district should not be used as a platform for religious expression.

Now you should have a pile of credentials from candidates that have passed the first test. For those of you professional leaders who have not been exposed to this process before, you will be shocked at how big the "no" pile is right now just after applying some common sense to the weeding-out process. The next document to look at in the suggested sequence requested is the resume. Look for candidates that have graduated from universities known for the education programs they provide and set them aside. This does not always mean that the large universities are better. In fact, the really good professional leaders usually do not graduate from the larger, well-known universities. Set them aside for now; however, this should only be done as a point of reference later.

This part should not weed anyone else out. Like the drafts for the National Football League, Major League Baseball, the National Basketball Association, and other major sporting organizations, sometimes the very best candidates have come from the most unknown places. Though this could be a deciding factor later in the hiring process, it is just something to keep in mind for now.

Look for experiences both in and out of education. However, don't be turned off by a lack of experience in education. Many districts now favor candidates coming right out of undergraduate schools strictly as a matter of fiscal responsibility. They are cheaper. However, there are a multitude of other obvious benefits from employing a candidate with a limited amount of experience in education. They may have a long-term loyalty to you and to the district for giving them their first chance. More importantly, there is a strong chance that the candidate will bring a fresh perspective and enthusiasm that cannot be replicated by candidates with experience.

When looking at experience outside of education, look for something specific. A very strong selling point should be the existence of experience in manual labor, working in a factory, or working in the food service industry, or any of those types of things. I know, I know, they have nothing to do with education, right? Wrong. Remember, you are looking for the right professional leader and the right person. Don't you want to know about things that are hard or next to impossible to interview for?

Things like work ethic, dedication, loyalty to the district, appreciation for what they have, and gratefulness for what they are about to potentially get. The professional leaders, just as a general rule, who have struggled at some time in their life, are the ones who will not only do anything to get the job, but will do anything to keep the job, regardless of tenure down the road. This is a minor thing on paper that may reveal a candidate will be appreciative of what they have, but even more so, grateful for their future if you give them the key to open that door. I'll bet that when you are looking for a professional leader who will be exceptional in the field, these are the kinds of things you are looking for in the *person* that gets hired.

There is one other reason why it is sometimes important that a candidate has experience with manual labor. In my experience, it is the candidate who has been exposed to manual labor that a district has a much better chance of elevating through professional development to the highest level of professional leadership. No research has been done on this that I know of. It could be argued that the effectiveness of this practice is predicated on a hunch and I would have no argument to that. Call it common sense. But in my experience this theory in practice has never failed.

Other important experiences to look for on a resume include service or volunteer experiences such as working at camps, retirement homes, and so on. Contrary to what was stated in the theory section about the First Amendment, it is in this one area where seeing something related to religion might not only be appropriate, but can be a selling point—things like church-related activities. Why are all of these things important? When you are looking for a top notch professional leader that is also a good person, it is in this area where you may be able to find those indicators on paper. With the right listings here, you may notice a person who is both passionate and compassionate. A person who is willing to work for free if they are doing something they love. This should also tell you that they might be willing to work on committees related to successful school change or volunteer to chaperone a dance without an expectation of payment for services. They will likely do these things for free because they will know when they get into this profession that these are the things that come with the territory. They will not feel entitled like many of their peers working in other professional fields. Rather, there is a great chance that they will be grateful for the opportunity to show and to prove that they will shine working in your district.

There is one other thing to look for on a resume before we move on to letters of recommendation. In the variety of experiences and background information, you may be interested in knowing in which of those listings the candidate performed in a leadership role and in which of them was he or she successful in working with others as a part of a team. Though they are not exclusionary things, they are helpful to know before an interview, not only to ask about in an interview, but for future reference if they are hired. You must know your professional leaders before you can implement successful school change. More on that later.

It is important to note who the letters of recommendation are coming from. It is generally understood that a good principal has a way of writing and interpreting a letter of recommendation in such a way that he or she can tip off to another principal who reads the letter where areas of concern may lie, without the candidate having any suspicions. The absence of a letter of recommendation from a principal should send up red flags. If you have a really good professional leader that you also think is a great person who does not have that letter, at the very least be sure to ask about the absence of that letter over the telephone or in person.

The absence of this letter can be explained. Maybe the principal never saw him or her teach. Maybe the candidate taught in a large district and hardly ever saw the principal, even after requesting an evaluation. Maybe the candidate asked the principal and the principal never got around to it. These are all fine explanations. However, there are a lot of explanations the candidate could give for the absence of that letter that might also make me raise my eyebrows.

I've never put a lot of stock into the letters from university professors. Nothing against them, they are wonderful people, too. Everyone knows that it is in the professor's best interests and in the university's best interests that as many of their students get jobs as possible. It is for this reason that I struggle to think of a time when a professor wrote even a questionable letter of recommendation for a student. In addition you should always call a supervisory teacher when he or she provides a letter of recommendation. You can sometimes tell over the phone if you ask the right questions and pay attention to tone, whether that person's letter will stand up or if he or she just wrote the letter to be nice.

A principal I know does something very unique in looking at candidate transcripts that might just be common sense to me, but I will relay it here anyway. She looks for an anomaly, something that stands out in a negative way. And it is usually easy to find an anomaly on college transcripts, for example, one B in a history of As. Why is this important? How could this possibly make a difference in a potential candidate? To be honest, it may not.

However, what you should be looking for on paper in good professional leaders is a sign that at some point in their life they have struggled. This is similar to the argument about the presence of manual labor listed on their previous job experience. You may be interested to know how they have learned and how they have had to overcome and persevere. That is the professional leader that will be able to relate to all staff and all students, not just the gifted ones. Many principals want a professional leader that is capable of putting themselves in someone else's shoes and, more specifically, into the shoes of a student or a staff member that struggles.

When you ask the candidate about the low grade on a transcript, considering him or her for hire might partially depend on the response to that question. It might make me wonder if the blame for the low grade were placed on someone or something else. However, if he or she takes ownership and can explain how they learned from the situation and were able to move on, then that may be the candidate I'm interested in. Let me be clear. I didn't say this argument should exclude those candidates that have gotten straight As as they are probably top notch candidates as well and maybe even more so. I just said it was something to look for and to pay attention to.

After going through this process and initial interview screening, you should have narrowed your pile down to five to ten that you are ready to interview.

So let's talk about interview questions. Here is where this process diverts drastically from best practices in interviewing. The interview should involve one person, usually the principal, creating his or her own list of questions that are unique to every position being hired.

Never use canned questions. Ever. Canned questions can never address the day to day issues that candidates will face and can never cover how they will respond to those issues.

Before the interview, be certain that a bank of questions center around both personal and professional answers related to the future and how the candidates see themselves fitting into your district's future. There should be a bank of questions that takes the candidates down a road of situations where they will have to reveal how they will respond to situations in the answers they give.

For example, you might ask a candidate to give an example of a situation in which he or she might send a student to the office. The answer you are looking for is one that involves a disruption in the normal flow of the classroom. You might then ask what the teacher would do if a student says FU when the teacher asks the student to go to the office. You are probably not concerned with that answer, as entertaining as it might be. The follow-up questions are where your interest might really lie. Later that student's parent calls the teacher and wants to know what the teacher did about another student who was disrupting class that day. This line of questioning could go on all day. Take the idea and make the questions and the answers you're looking for match whatever the need is for the position you are hiring.

Remember that by going through this process, you will truly get to know a candidate. You will be fully aware of what you are getting as a professional leader and as a person before he or she is hired. Just like in the days of the one-room schoolhouse. Remember though that two other things could happen during the interview process. The first is that it may become very apparent within fifteen minutes that you have a home run candidate. Jump on it, but jump the right way — cautiously.

The second thing that could happen is that you may have a round of duds. If you are not on a strict timeline, and most districts most times are not, repost the position and start again. There is a very strong chance that after it is posted a second time, potential high-quality professional leaders who were in the "no" pile the first go around will have corrected the minor error that put them there (if they don't already have a job). Posting the same job a second time is not defeat. This is called raising the bar. If you know the professional leader and the kind of person you want, you will get it. Do not settle. Though it may be a pain in the butt to go through it all again, if you raise the bar, you will get what you want. Unfortunately, if you lower the bar and settle, you will also get what you deserve. We owe it to our students to raise the bar.

This chapter began with a great interviewing story, and a true one at that. Sometimes you get a round of duds and you may want to cut off an interview before it even begins. In my first year as a principal I had this experience. The candidate came into the office wearing a real flower in her hair. She assumed that I was a teacher. I began making small talk to try to get a feel for the kind of person she was. She began telling me about the Grateful Dead concert she had been to the weekend before in which she was involved with smoking a significant amount of marijuana.

She then proceeded to tell me the story of how the flower got in her hair. While student teaching that day, a third grader in her class picked the flower for her while out at recess. The student teacher put it in her hair because the flower reminded her of a time when she dropped acid with her boyfriend recently. She also mentioned that she told the student that picked the flower this story as well while thanking her for the flower. She was very surprised to learn that I was the principal and that she would not really be participating in an interview that day.

CONCLUSION

I could go on about this hiring business forever. If you have any further questions about the hiring process outlined here, if you need more detail about initial interview screening over the telephone, types of questions to ask, what to listen for, how to offer a job, or any other thing, shoot me an e-mail at joedawidziak@gmail.com. Because of the length of this chapter, it is the only one with a conclusion. It is necessary, not only to reiterate the points made in the chapter but to clarify why following the hiring process outlined here may be best practice for your district, even when it is clearly not best practice in education today.

There are many contradictions in this chapter and I am aware of that. Hiring can be a weird business in which something that works for one situation may not for another. These are only guidelines that have been found to work sometimes. Despite what experts might tell, there is no surefire way to do it so that you are guaranteed to get the best candidate every time. I will tell you though that if you want a great teacher and a great person, there are some things here to consider.

In chapter 1 of her book *Improving Student Learning One Teacher at a Time* (2007), Jane Pollock discusses the notion of replacing hope with certainty. I believe that following this hiring process to get the right fit puts districts in a position to do exactly that. It gives districts the best chance of hiring not just a sure thing, but a sure thing that is also a good person. Working off of that same idea, it can also be argued that when working with difficult teachers, professional leaders should consider the notion of replacing consequences and punishment with professional development. I never used to believe in this when I first became a principal, but it is a rule to live by now. Especially if you want them to help you with successful school change later down the road.

If a teacher is poor and is always going to be poor, there will be time for documentation and consequences later. Those professional leaders will continue to make the same mistakes regardless of the professional development a district may provide. However, if a teacher is poor and willing to be better, by providing professional development instead of consequences and punishment, then you have most likely found yourself a diamond in the rough.

There is a chapter titled "Focusing on Success" in Daniel Johnson's book *Sustaining Change in Schools* (2005) that begins with the line "Success begins with a change in expectations. It is sustained with a change in attitudes." What an incredibly accurate description of successful school change, especially for districts that are not used to change. This is why chapter 5 is so important.

What Mr. Johnson suggests is paralleled here, which is to say that if you want to change attitudes, you must first change expectations. I'm not one to use sports analogies frequently when it comes to an academic agenda, but it is here where one is truly relevant. There are several sports teams that have been losing for a very long time. The teams that have been able to change things have done so not only by hiring the best talent out there, but by getting their existing teams to change how they think. It is crucial before anyone can win, whether in sports or in education, for those that call the shots to raise the bar of their own expectations and get professional leaders to think they *can* win.

All of the advice here is to be used as a guideline. There are two important things to take from this chapter; one is simple, the other is not. The first is that even in the cases where the word "teacher" is used, remember all of the advice on hiring provided here is intended to be applied to all professional leaders, including administrators. The second point is that all of the things discussed here can only be accomplished with an interview done in a face-to-face, one on one situation.

This means the person representing the district had better be good, had better be trusted, and had better have a great knowledge of exactly the right fit that is needed for that particular situation. This means understanding that sometimes you need an excellent professional leader with a particular character trait, whereas in another situation you may need an excellent professional leader who can be a follower. In either situation, the person in charge of the hiring and interview process ends up with an excellent professional leader who is also an excellent person. And for better or worse, in most situations, that person in charge who really knows the right fit that is needed in a school district is typically the principal.

CHAPTER 4

The Train Is Leaving the Station

THE STORY

A favorite story in education sometimes used by professional leaders involves "the train leaving the station." A district in Iowa was having a struggle with getting a group of teachers on board with district initiatives. At the time there were several district initiatives that this group of teachers was not cooperating with. Professional leaders in the district had tried the nice, soft approach. They had tried the in-between approach. Finally, they tried the stern approach. The situation was already reaching a boiling point when they used "the train leaving the station" story.

The professional leaders in Iowa helped their teachers to understand by talking about the train story as if it were an unrelated tale. They explained that the train was leaving the station. The uncooperative professional leaders could be on the train or they could be off the train. Either way, the train was leaving. The professional leaders explained further that they really wanted the uncooperative professional leaders to be on the train with them. However, it was explained clearly that if the professional leaders were going to stand in front of the train, the train would not be stopping. The discussion was concluded by asking the professional leaders if it was their intent to be on the train, off the train, or in front of the train, explaining that the answer they were about to give would allow those promoting change in the district to plan accordingly.

THE THEORY

There is a saying that a lot of professional school leaders are very fond of using: "If you are not moving forward, you are moving backward." As pointed out in chapter 1, stagnancy promotes getting caught in the trap of success. Simply put, this is the theory behind chapter 4. In education, as we all know, if you remain stagnant as a professional leader or as a district, that equates to moving backward. Also applicable to the PreK–12 educational system is the University of Wisconsin motto "Forward, Thinking." If you are not always thinking about planning for the future, you are thinking too much about the past. Reminiscing and knowing what has worked in the past are healthy habits, but obsessing about the past can be a poisonous one.

There is a theory out there that the concept of merit pay will get everyone on the train. Not true. In fact, it will do more to divide those who are on the train and those who are not. Despite what some politicians and business leaders strive for, professional leaders should never consider the concept of merit pay as valid. Forget data and research and best practice right here. The following story is a great example of why what you are about to read here is real, practical, commonsense advice.

During a discussion with a local principal, a professional "expert" in the field of education directed a question as to why the principal never followed through with some of her very sound, very practical ideas for school change. The principal stated a fact that she was concerned about disrupting the wonderful working environment that had taken years to establish with professional leaders. She was concerned that the environment would be jeopardized if she initiated steps for change before the other professional leaders were ready.

The expert asked the principal how she knew when the other professional leaders were ready. The principal responded with "when they are all on the train." The educational expert felt the need to explain with two more questions after she had laughed out loud at the response to the first. How long will you wait before you decide whether or not they are all on the train? What will you do when you realize that a minority will never be on the train no matter how long you wait? These two questions propelled the entire discussion to go down a different track.

The principal expressed her primary concern that she didn't want to change the environment into one in which professional leaders show up and leave at the contracted times and put forth no extra effort. In return the expert explained that though they were in the minority, the professional leaders who wouldn't be on the train were already showing up and leaving at the contracted times and putting forth no extra effort. Those professional leaders who are at school for all the right reasons will still continue to work just as hard regardless of the steps for change that may be implemented. Those are the professional leaders in education that are the definition of true professionals.

There is a subtle point here that the expert was trying to get across to the principal in this story that will be made more obvious now. The true professional leaders that are good at their jobs in education will always be good no matter what the circumstances. Regardless of the change around them, the pressure, the amount of students in their classes, or the behavioral issues in their classes, they will continue to perform at the highest possible level. These are the professional leaders that will perform at an extremely high level whether they have thirty-five kids in their room or two, whether they have a large, luxurious classroom with all the amenities or whether they are teaching in a closet. They will be on the train and stay on it even if you are driving it into the side of a mountain. It is also those professionals that will steer the train and divert it from crashing into the side of a mountain and deliver the district to the promised land.

It is for this reason that merit pay in education means nothing. If there are professional leaders that respect their boss, they will run through a wall for them without ever being given a raise or asking if it hurt or not. If there are professional leaders that do not respect their boss, some of them will never sign up for a committee or stay after the contracted time, even if you offered them a million dollars to do so. And guess what? The same thing is true of our students. Because of this, merit pay only works in the business world. In education, it only encourages the hoarding of resources, the promoting of jealousy and envy, and the creating of incentives for the proliferation of individuals working alone for selfish reasons. The idea of merit pay takes away from the collaborative process that has taken education years to achieve.

After reading chapter 3 you understand how critical it is to hire the right people and an example of a little-used process to do so. Now that you've hired the right people, the next process involves weeding out those who are not on board the train or motivating them to be on board the train, with an emphasis on the latter. The explanation of the theory of how to do this can get a little tricky and there is sometimes no politically correct, comfortable way to express it. For professional leaders who are the type of people that like to sometimes tell it the way they see it, this can get them in trouble from time to time.

When schools need to make a change or start a new initiative, there is always going to be a person or a group of people who will want to resist no matter how much sense it may make to the rest of the world. That is okay and a good, healthy scenario for progress. However, sometimes, at some point someone needs to tell them the way it is. The train analogy may be the best way to do that. The problem is that the recipient of that message, because of the nature of the recipient, probably will not receive the message in a positive light, particularly if the message does not come across in a positive light.

When new change is ready to occur, the group of professionals receiving the news of the change falls into one of three categories: those that are on the train, those that are not on the train, and those that are in front of the train. The only thing that usually distinguishes the difficulty of transition from one change to another is the amount of people in each of those three categories. The source of concern that stands in the way of progress and change isn't the group that is not on the train; it is the group that is in front of the train.

THE PRACTICE

Let's take these issues one at a time, with the easiest first. That would be working with those professional leaders that are already on the train. Sue is someone who is on the train. She might ask a lot of questions when she receives the news of an upcoming initiative, but she isn't likely to gossip or do side conversations at faculty meetings. Sure, she might notice contradictions in features of the initiative, but her concerns are of a logical and rational nature. She isn't opposed just to be oppositional. If you've done the right preparatory work and have followed some commonsense guidelines, the majority of the group will be in this category. If the groundwork has been laid and the timing is right, the only challenge here will be keeping them on the train. There are various means to do that including challenge, motivation, and continually piquing the interest level.

Some professional leaders simply need to be challenged. Some thrive on being able to prove others wrong. So tell them it can't be done. John is a teacher who isn't good at taking orders and certainly doesn't like being told what to do. He has gotten to where he is today by being very good at finding ways to beat the system. I promise you that if you tell John it cannot be done, John will find a way to get it done.

Some thrive on being told it can be done. So tell them they can do it. Some thrive on being asked if they think they can do it. So ask them if they can do it. The important part here is knowing the professional leader well enough to know which questions are appropriate for which professional leaders. A mistake in making the appropriate challenge obviously can become a barrier sooner and later.

Motivating adults is shockingly similar to motivating students. Some professional leaders will produce because they are intrinsically motivated. Tell them they are doing a good job and encourage them along the way. Some professional leaders are extrinsically motivated. Bribe them with something. Some professional leaders are complicated and may need both. So give them both. And the rare ones, much like some of our gifted students, need no motivation at all.

Throughout the process of successful school change professional leaders must remind each other why the change is important. How does it help students? Remind each other how it helps the district. Remind each other during the process why you are doing this and how great it will be when it is done. Remind each other why you got into the game of education to begin with. Again, to motivate adults properly, just like students, you must know them well enough to know what is appropriate for the group as a whole and for individuals. And as any expert will tell you, celebrate when you get there. But now we are getting way ahead of ourselves.

The second challenge in this process is dealing with those who may be in the station but are not on the train. Their reasons may be legitimate, but with the proper nudging they can typically be swayed one way or the other. This is done using data, real-world successful case studies in districts similar to yours, time, and yes, sometimes incentives or bribery, whichever one of those terms you prefer. Many of those not on the train have been on the wrong train before, one that was constantly late or one that broke down. They might be leery of getting on another train. Help them to want to take another ride.

Most of the professional leaders on the fence do not need warm fuzzies. They want real-world proof that this is the right thing to do. So give them data and research, particularly from districts similar to yours, and follow up. Create a pilot group in your district well ahead of schedule on the timeline that you'd like to see the real change actually happen. Then give those on the fence the data and the research from your own district that shows it will be successful and what is best for your own students in your own district. There is no more powerful data than that. And if all else fails and you have to use incentives or bribery, so be it. It is what it is.

The third challenge and the most challenging is working with the very small group that is front of the train. Sometimes they are active; sometimes they are passive. Either way, the solution can be unusually easy or extremely difficult. There are two approaches, and though both could be done simultaneously, both should be done very slowly.

The first approach is to remind them that the train will go on whether they are on it or not. As long as they are not in front of the train but watching it pass by, tell them you are okay with that, whether you are or not. And do this tactfully and in a positive light. It will be the difference between getting them aboard later and never getting them aboard at all. After that, say nothing and do nothing. Time and their own observations will take care of the rest. This is the group that doesn't just need to see proof and data; they need to see the proof and data in action. Then they will come around and that is okay and that is healthy. Because once they are on board after this they will likely never get off again. They have been convinced.

The second approach is much more difficult and could be done simultaneously with the first. Unfortunately, it involves documentation and a lot of it. Remember, this is only for those standing in front of the train, not for those standing in the train station. And also know that there is more than a 50/50 chance that this too will not be successful. It still depends on it being done in a positive light. It still depends on reminding them why it is important for the district and what is best for kids. And most importantly, they need to be reminded why they are a critical part in the process and why it cannot be successful without their help. At first, professional leaders don't always have to be willing to act but they do need to be willing to listen. If you get them to listen, you can get them to act later.

Have a plan for when the train breaks down. If you are a professional leader, have the expectation that it will break down and have a plan. It probably won't break down, but have a plan anyway. The good professional leaders always do. Once you have hired all the right professional leaders and you have all the new and existing professional leaders on the same page and ready to move in the same direction, the most critical element comes next. It is one that will permanently keep professional leaders on the same page, even if they don't always agree with district professional leaders or the changes they propose. I don't mean for this one change deemed necessary right now, but for all school change to follow for the rest of their careers. I'll bet I've got your attention now. That's right, there is one thing that can keep even your bitter enemies, be it other professional leaders or students, on your side for the duration of both of your careers. It is showing you care.

CHAPTER 5

Well, Well, Well

THE STORY

While sitting in a doctoral class one day, the professor told the class an interesting and classic story. As a youngster, the professor was paddled as a first grader in Oklahoma for having too many pairs of scissors in his desk as a result of forgetting to pass them forward after activities. I guess in those days it wasn't just the nuns in Catholic schools that had interesting ways of keeping order. A student in this class wondered out loud if, after some time passes and after teachers and administrators retire, they spend the rest of their lives regretting those incidents. Particularly after society has changed and after having time away from education to think about their actions over their careers?

Are educators haunted by their experiences after they retire? Are they spending time thinking about what could have been or what should have been or what might have been? Are they wondering what they could or should have done differently in certain situations? And more importantly, are these thoughts interfering with the time that should be spent relaxing and enjoying retirement? Do professional leaders have regrets after they retire? You betcha, especially the ones who were really good in their day.

THE THEORY

As any good professional leader will learn, all successful school change occurs and is sustained as a result of the efforts of those in the trenches on a day-to-day basis. Research shows that this requires that those professional leaders feel like they are working toward something, for the greater good, and for someone they trust and respect. They must feel as if they are cared for and cared about. They must feel like their own overall wellness is a concern to those they are working for.

For this reason, districts should be spending the same amount of time, resources, energy, and money on professionals preparing to exit the profession as they do on the professionals entering it. Reality tells us that given the financial state of districts today this theory may never come to full fruition in our time as is about to be suggested in this chapter. But there are still certain things that can be done to ensure a state of tranquility for retired employees, regardless of finances.

Why is this chapter important? Now that you have all the right people in place, have cleaned the kitchen, and have everyone with a general understanding and moving in the direction the district wants to go, it is critical that you show you care about them. Gary Vaynerchuk (2009) dedicates an entire chapter of his book *Crush It!* to this notion that is summed up in one word in his book: *care*. When you show you care about your employees, it isn't just the little things you should be concerned about. Not just the things like asking about their families, friends, and pets. It is actually caring about them long term, both while they are employed and while they are retired. If you hired the right person, the sincere caring you show is for life, not just for their career. This chapter provides some insight into how school districts and all fields can care for their employees on a larger and much deeper scale.

Almost every district has a wellness policy, but very few address the important ideas of retirement mentoring and career debriefing. Not retirement planning, retirement mentoring. Why is this distinction important? Because districts that truly care about their employees should continue to do so even after they are retired. And why is that important? Because districts who care about their employees after they are retired understand that it is important to be concerned about taking care of those who have taken care of the district. In doing so, you will have employees who will work for school change at a frenetic pace while they are still employed because they will know they can truly relax after they are retired.

Common sense will tell you that employees that have either endured successful school change or, more importantly, embraced it and been its ambassador for the district during their entire careers should be rewarded for the stress of the sometimes high-stakes game they have been playing for so many years. These are the professional leaders that a successful district is founded on and many of their most important efforts over the years will have gone unpaid simply because they have been professional leaders and that is what is expected of them.

There is a connection that can be made between research and the assumption that there should be an importance placed on implementing a process of mentoring for professional educators prior to retirement, similar to the process of mentoring initial educators after they are hired. Research in the areas of the mentoring process, the effects of retirement on disposition, and the effectiveness of career debriefing also indicates a need for the development of retirement mentoring programs for educators.

Providing retirement mentoring should be viewed as a way for school districts to show concern for the long-term health and well-being of exiting professional educators, similar to a long-term district wellness plan. There are several points that provide insight and outline several factors that will contribute to the idea of establishing retirement mentoring programs as viable and needed in the field of education. It is necessary to further reveal why it is important for the field of education to consider how the establishment of retirement mentoring programs would be a benefit to the future retiree, the school district, and the field of education as a whole.

First, let's talk about the mentoring process. The Greek version of the word "mentor" translates into "enduring." Most professional educators define a mentor as it relates to new teachers as a person who has a supportive role procedurally, morally, socially, and emotionally and provides resources, knowledge, and feedback and engages the mentee in reflective thinking. This same definition holds true for veteran professional educators about to retire, and they would require those same services from a mentor who is already retired.

What is interesting is that the word mentor itself, especially the Greek translation, lends itself to the understanding that the process should be intended to be provided over the course of a long time. Historically in education, however, a mentor is only provided for a short amount of time and at the beginning of a professional leader's career. After this, it's as if it is no longer necessary.

Whether provided for a short or a long time, for initial educators or master educators, the overall success of a mentoring program hinges on the relationship between the mentor and the mentee, rather than on transfer of skills and dispositions. In Bolman and Deal's (1997) *Reframing Organizations*, the authors argue that the premise of mentoring is founded on the basis of interpersonal dynamics and the humanistic characteristics of the relationship between mentor and mentee. There is a human element to a proper mentoring process that is critical to its success. In layman's terms, the mentee and the mentor have to like each other. They have to get along. Just sitting together and talking isn't good enough. There has to be some give and take in the relationship and in the discussion that has a deeper meaning, and this must happen for the process to be successful.

As suggested by Sergiovanni and Starratt (2002) in their book *Supervision: A Redefinition*, the mentor-mentee relationship begins to mature and develop into a reciprocal professional development opportunity for both parties. It is when this is achieved that the true spirit of the mentoring process lends itself to professional development and eventually school change. This occurs because people talk. In your district, they will begin talking about this mentoring process you have started. Why not get the chatter going in the right direction?

Those participating in the process will tell others how positive and productive it was and how grateful they are to the district for providing it. Once the program is established, professional leaders in your district will begin looking forward to participating in school change because they will want to get to this great place at the end of their career where they are taken care of for the enjoyment of their retirement.

Let's take that idea one step further. Districts that implement a retirement mentoring program should advertise it as a trade-off and make it known that it is provided as a reward for professional leaders embracing school change throughout their careers. It should be talked about during the interview and hiring process when new professional leaders are hired. New hires should know what to look forward to in initially getting a job in your district, but also that there is a reward at the end as well.

Providing mentoring for initial educators entering the field of education has clearly become a common practice in education as a result of legislation and good practice. It could be argued loosely that mentoring could act as a basic human need for professional leaders, especially at high stress points in the course of life and careers, for example, when entering or exiting the profession. Mentoring is viewed as a positive contributor to teacher retention. If given the chance, mentoring could also be viewed as a positive contributor to happiness in retirement.

The principles pertaining to mentoring that are described in research suggest that good mentoring also goes beyond a moment in time. If there is a significant relationship between the mentor and the mentee and between the district and its employees, the mentoring process itself becomes a part of a caring culture. That caring culture does not end when the initial educator becomes a professional educator. The caring that a district shows for its professional leaders should not end when the professional leader retires, regardless of their role in the field of education.

It would make sense then that if a connection can be established between research and theory, that taking action and creating a plan would be the next step. If mentoring is clearly a good practice for professional leaders transitioning into the field, it could certainly be argued that it may be an equally sound practice to provide a mentoring process for those professional educators exiting the field. It is a way to show the district *cares* about its professional leaders.

Most professional leaders in education are left exposed out on an island in a high-profile role for a very long time over the course of their careers. When professional leaders first begin a retirement mentoring program in a district, there is a need for both retired educators and those about to retire, to fill an emotional and social void. This is a void created by either the absence of the high-profile role they used to have or what is about to be an absence if they are about to retire.

A friend once told me that in her experience working in the Chicago public school system, professional leaders spent much more time planning things like vacations, birthday parties, and holidays than they ever did with their own retirement. As a result of poor planning, retirees from education are not happy during their retirement. This seems contradictory to the reason some professional leaders retire to begin with, which is to experience happiness, enjoyment, and relaxation after a long, hard career in a demanding, high-profile role.

As a professional leader in your district, ask yourself, do you care about your colleagues? How much? Do you care enough about them to want to make them happy *after* they retire? I didn't ask you if you liked them all; I asked if you cared about them all. These are two very different things. Do you care enough to want to do that? You should. Otherwise, either you do not have the right people working with you or you are the problem that needs to be removed. If you are struggling to understand this, remember what was said in chapters 2 and 4. If you care, then let the school change happen and be a supporter and a promoter. If you do not care, then let the change happen without you and move on to another district or another profession.

This suggests that retirees in education, due to the combination of a lack of a retirement mentoring program and their own lack of preparation, are ill prepared for their future as retirees socially, psychologically, and emotionally. This concerns me because I wonder if their disposition during retirement changes negatively due to the lack of preparation before retirement. What this means is I wonder if some retirees are not enjoying their retirement because they are spending too much time worrying about regrets and things that they would have, should have, could have done, or did not do.

Satisfaction during retirement is also partly dependent upon the state of mind the soon-to-be retiree is in just before they are about to retire. Professional leaders who leave the field in a state of stress, distress, bitterness, or anger are probably going to spend their retirement years wondering. And those retirees will probably spend at least some of their retirement in the same state of mind that they were in when they left the field. Those professional leaders leaving the field on their own terms and after having participated in a retirement mentoring program are more likely to be happy, and continue to be happy and relaxed in retirement with no regrets.

The theory suggested here is that it is important that school districts consider providing retirement mentoring programs in order to ensure the wellness, health, and positive disposition of potential retirees after retirement. There is clearly a need for retirement mentoring programs not only in the field of education but in other professional fields as well. Curl and Townsend (2008), along with Sternberg (2004), suggest in their research that the absence of retirement mentoring programs and mandated retirement planning could potentially have an adverse effect on the disposition of retirees after retirement. It can be assumed from their research that institutions cannot simply assume employee happiness and satisfaction after retirement due to the act of retirement alone. It can be assumed also that the implementation of retirement mentoring programs needs to be varied in intensity.

The studies that have been done on the very few companies that have provided at least some aspects of retirement mentoring programs (though they are not called retirement mentoring programs and do not include all the components of a retirement mentoring program) have all found the same theory to be true. That providing the programs *before* retirement has profound effects on disposition and the overall wellness of the retiree.

Let me let you in on a little commonsense reason why you should care and why you should start to consider implementation of a retirement mentoring program, but also the idea of career debriefing in that program, as a way to sincerely show you care. Professional leaders in most districts, but especially in the inner cities' ones, over time develop a battlefield focus and a battlemind type of thinking. Those professional leaders, by the time they retire, are in full survival mode. They themselves don't realize that they do not think the same way that they did when they entered the field. We owe it to our professional leaders who have served so long and so well to give them their minds back and give them back their ability to relax—much like the military owes it to battle-tested soldiers returning from war, as unrelated as that analogy might appear to be.

In considering the idea of providing retirement mentoring programs in education, a key component of those programs would be the inclusion of the idea of career debriefing. This is a concept that has already been taken up to some degree in several other professional fields, including the medical, legal, and law enforcement fields. It is common knowledge that the concept of debriefing originated in the military. However, it has been further developed by the military and by other fields for use in other areas since its creation.

This process or program that I've been talking about really boils down to talking. In the military they say that leaving a soldier with his or her own thoughts after a stressful event is the most critical mistake. You must get them to talk about their experiences to heal the mind again. The idea of simple "talk" is the most important factor in reestablishing morale. It is that talk that you provide both during successful school change and during retirement mentoring that will create chatter in the right direction for the entire district as well. More about getting the right kind of chatter going for the benefit of successful school change later.

Though debriefing was not originally intended as a stress reliever, that ended up being the most positive and effective result of the process. This clearly has implications for the importance of its use in the implementation of a career debriefing process within a retirement mentoring program provided for professional leaders in the field of education and in many other fields as well. As in other professional fields, professional leaders are quick to feel blame or embarrassment if they feel like mistakes in their careers are their own fault. So it is also important in providing retirement programs with the inclusion of career debriefing that the process be set up in a risk-free environment, similar to the environment we would expect professional leaders to set up for their own students in their own classrooms.

Are you still with me? All of this means that professional leaders may be very stressed out at the end of their careers without ever knowing it, without ever knowing that the level of stress they have achieved over the years may have an adverse affect on their disposition after retirement. I feel confident in saying the one of the biggest reasons professional leaders may be stressed out at the end of their careers is because they have been a part of, or the promoters for, successful school change for decades. And to help them get over the stress can be so easy. Show them you *care*.

THE PRACTICE

Okay, so maybe you were thinking this book wasn't so bad until we got to this chapter with all of its technicalities. By now you might be saying, "Give me the English version, please." If you want school change to be successful and long lasting, love your employees. Care about them not with words, but also with actions. Care about them not just for their careers, but for the duration of their lives. Prepare them not just to lead professionally, but to retire. What else is there that will motivate professional leaders more than knowing they will be taken care of, not for their careers, but for their lives? That kind of confidence and security leads to wanting to be a part of continuous growth and change that is unsurpassed. Not just for them as an individual, but by default, for the entire district as a whole.

If you ever get to the point of implementing retirement planning in your district, remember that there are a few critical elements. First, like any mentoring, the relationship is what makes mentoring successful and valuable, not just the process or saying that you've implemented the process. The second is to make it an absolute requirement that career debriefing is a part of the retirement mentoring process. The military uses it, the legal field uses it, the medical field uses it, and so do other fields. Are we not professionals? Are we not leaders? Isn't it just common sense that we might take what works in retirement mentoring for other professional fields and use it in the one field that is truly professional?

Education is providing mentoring to new professional leaders at various degrees of effectiveness, mostly the result of various acts of legislation. As a result leaders in education often deal with a multitude of issues related to mentoring professional leaders entering the field. What should be considered equally important is preparing educational professionals with retirement mentoring as they are leaving the profession. Remember, I didn't say retirement planning, I said retirement mentoring. This concept of retirement mentoring has little to do with finances. It is preparing them for the enjoyment of the next stage of their lives because you sincerely *care* about them.

Michael Fullan (2008) in his book *The Six Secrets of Change* believes that school districts should love their employees. The concept of loving your employees doesn't just apply to the length of their careers, but to the length of their lives. You've heard that over and over again in this chapter. Despite this, it could be implied with the philosophy of professional development to this point in education that we really only love our professional leaders more in the beginning and the middle of their careers than at the end or after their careers are over.

This also rings true when you begin to examine where all of the money goes and the professional development that takes place in the career of an educator. All the time, effort, resources, and money are spent in the formative years for initial educators, and in the middle years for the professional or master educators that you want to improve and who want to be continuously professionally developed. Little time, money, or consideration is spent evaluating the importance of preparing educators mentally, socially, or psychologically before or after retirement. After the retirement party is over, the school district just moves on.

This is a big mistake we are making in education and we are missing a golden opportunity to change the mindset of the professional leaders in our districts about change and wanting to be a part of change for the greater good. And because we are missing the opportunity to change the mindset, we are missing a chance to use those professional leaders to develop a successful school change process that will last much longer than the lifespan of the employees and to set the tone for generations of professional leaders to come in our school districts. As a result of not placing enough emphasis on caring for our employees to create a successful change environment, we look for other substitutes. We can fall into the mistake of thinking that money will then be the answer to successful school change. As you may already know and as you will find out further in chapter 6, fixing something with money is not a reality for most professional leaders in education.

CHAPTER 6

Money Is the Answer—To Nothing

THE STORY

Several years ago when a small district in Tennessee was in tight financial straits, the new administration started the year with an all-staff meeting, as is probably the case with just about every other school across the country on the first day of in-service or teacher institutes. During this meeting, the administration explained that they no longer wanted to hear what couldn't be done because they didn't have the money. Instead, they issued a challenge to their staff to create a list of what they did want to accomplish. Then the administrators challenged themselves to show the teachers that they could make it happen, regardless of the expense.

The purpose for the message was twofold. Initially, they wanted to change the long-entrenched negative mindset the staff had regarding the district's financial situation. The administration wanted to find a new way to turn a negative mindset into a positive one with no ammunition other than knowledge. This was a necessary thing because the teachers in the district had gotten used to the idea that they were inhibited by money, or a lack thereof.

The second reason for the message was to find ways to prove that the presence of money in a budget really doesn't solve any problems or facilitate any change. Trust me, there is a lot of research to support that idea if you are interested in finding it. There is also research to support the idea that successful decision making relies heavily on having the right people in place, not money. As discussed in chapters 3, 4, and 5, if you've got the right fit, everyone is in place, and everyone is moving

59

in the same direction, you can accomplish anything. Common sense tells us that getting the right fit is wonderful, but there must be more. Having the right mindset is the true key to change and to success, as addressed in chapters 2, 4, and 5. These are all things that money cannot buy and that money cannot help with.

THE THEORY

Simply put, money solves nothing. We hear stories of down-on-their-luck people winning the lottery or a small timer making it big in the entertainment industry. Those people, rightly so, have their moment in the sun and in the spotlight. However, when it is all said and done, some of those people just wish they could have their normal lives back. Too much money changes people and it changes institutions also. Too much money can, over time, change an individual's value system and the fundamental moral compass that should drive an institution's good decision making.

For those of you in Lake Forest, Illinois, and other school districts that have had money and continue to do wonderful things with it, keep in mind I said that money can change value systems and moral compass, not that it would. And for those districts that are really struggling financially, I am not saying that having money isn't helpful for real, long-lasting solutions. The point that will be made in this chapter is that any district, regardless of financial standing, that relies on money or uses it as an excuse, when there are so many other resources under our noses, might be making a mistake.

Many districts make a mistake in letting their employees believe that a lack of funding is an inhibitor to getting things accomplished. Not true. It can be argued that the lack of funding is the biggest catapult for creative thinking among professional leaders in education. Funding issues can actually be a major positive contributor to getting things done and facilitating school change. It forces creative thinkers to come up with alternatives to create success or initiate change. A lack of funding among the right group of people allows for more of a grassroots, underdog philosophy to change and to achieving educational success. And it is this kind of change and success that stands the test of time.

Another mistake a lot of districts and professional leaders make is waiting to take action or make changes until the district can afford it. There are theories out there that state that to implement change a district must be ready to eliminate something that already exists to keep the order of things, as referenced in chapter 3. Sometimes this is true; sometimes it isn't always necessarily true. Sometimes new things, including the process of change, and especially if it is done right, cannot wait for an elimination of something already existing. If people waited until they could afford to buy a home before they bought one, a very small minority of the population would be homeowners. If people waited until they could afford to have children before they had them, most of us in education would be out of a job. There are times when it is no different in education. You can't always afford to wait for the money or for the elimination of something existing to begin the process of implementing successful school change.

THE PRACTICE

If you are a professional leader in education, you already know that it is a disservice to allow your district to rest on its laurels in any capacity. This is not news to you. Accordingly, it is not okay to allow the excuse to seep into the minds of other professional leaders on any level that a lack of funding is an obstacle to change. It becomes the responsibility of good professional leaders to promote the exact opposite idea. Promote the idea that a lack of funding is actually the instigator of successful school change and to forward-thinking progress. This isn't just an idea you are promoting; it is reality.

The first question most district leaders face is this: What will you spend the little money you have on? Spending the little money we have on fads in education is a continuing and disturbing trend in education. Despite all of the things out there that should prevent this from happening, unfortunately, it still does. This often is allowed to happen in our field when there is an emphasis correctly placed on results, but the process of getting the results is either not considered at all, or is not considered correctly or accurately. In my own terms, this can more adequately and accurately be called *panic* emphasis. It would seem obvious that this sort of thing wouldn't happen in education so how can it be that it still does? This is a question to be examined.

In spending district money when funds are limited, it should only be spent on surefire, research proven, and time-tested things. Money in education should be spent on things that will stand the test of time. There are so many programs and other things that districts spend their money on that do not focus of the process of how to get results. Here are some commonsense things districts should be spending their money on that will stand up over the test of time: curriculum, school and professional libraries, professional development, and technology.

These are four areas that are constantly changing and have been critical elements to sustained long-term successful school change and improved or sustained student achievement. If school change can somehow legitimately fit into one of these four categories, it is usually a safe bet that you are on the right track. But buyer, beware. Just because something your district wants to buy fits into one of these four categories, that doesn't mean it stands up over the test of time. It also doesn't always mean it is what is best for your district, even though all the research out there might try to tell you it is. There has to be a much deeper meaning into a purchase.

Remember that when spending money on curriculum, not just any curriculum will do. In a time of financial crisis a district should focus all of their time, energy, and spending on reading and math first, everything else second. If you want to save money, do it in a content area that is not reading or math. Similar to concentrating efforts to raise standardized state test scores, these are the two key areas to spend money on. If you can get your hands around these two content areas, the rest will take care of itself.

Set aside funds for professional development, but remember to also dictate to staff how that money will be a return for everyone in the district, specifically students. Make sure they put in writing how the conference they want to attend ties to district goals. How does the class a professional leader wants to take line up with the district's mission? After any type of professional development, make sure there is a requirement that they report back what they have learned to the rest of the staff. Encourage them to donate any books that were bought for classes or for professional development to the district's own professional development library. This is a cheap and easy way to expand and develop your resources, especially for smaller schools and districts.

Technology is the single most important tool for leveling the playing field in education on a global scale. There are some who will argue it is good, and some who will argue that it is bad. Here, though, is one of the only safe bets in spending in education. Regardless of your opinion on the matter, it is not going away. It is just going to keep on advancing, whether it is bringing your district along for the ride or not. If you want your district to keep up in all areas of education, be sure to spend money here. It is one of the few ways to keep up with a changing new world that we should be preparing our students for, not preventing them from. Districts should be encouraged to always set aside a certain amount annually for spending in this area.

The answer to why districts in crisis continue spending money inaccurately is as easy as apple pie. It goes back to panic emphasis. Here is a typical example of how a struggling school might react. A school board sees declining test scores and tells its administration that the scores need to increase or they will lose their jobs. Professional leaders in the field know this cannot happen overnight, but board members, sometimes with little or no background in education, sometimes do not. So the administrators are left scrambling to come up with a quick fix. Not what is best for kids or the district, but maybe what is best to save their jobs or to make the district look better.

If you were in the same situation, maybe you cannot blame the administrators for looking for some program, workshop, or motivational speaker. Sometimes this works, not because the program, workshop, or speaker was successful in getting the desired student achievement results, but because the administration now has someone or something to blame when they do not get the results within the board's desired time frame. Panic emphasis happens all the time. It means you are finding something, anything, to stem the tide for now. Panic emphasis puts districts in survival mode, not achievement mode. However, it can also mean spending is occurring in places where it isn't necessary.

Here is a final note about money being an answer in education. As you start to change your thinking about using a lack of funding as a propellant instead of an inhibitor, remember this: though money can change a lot of things, positive and negative, it cannot force successful change to happen. Though you can change your own perception and the perceptions of those around you about the lack of money being an instigator instead of a barrier, there is another critical thing to remember. Sometimes for change to happen perceptions not having to do with money must first also be changed. And those perceptions are ones that money alone cannot change. Not in education.

CHAPTER 7

Perception vs. Reality

THE THREE STORIES

In the first year of teaching, a sixth-grade teacher came across a savvy, street-smart class clown student whom we will call "Mike." Mike was a student of average intelligence who had been identified as at risk. One day the teacher was explaining a concept using an overhead projector. Mike was closest to the light switch and the teacher asked him to please flick off the lights. As the teacher continued on with the lesson, he began to notice that the class was not paying attention to him as well as usual. In fact, they really weren't paying attention at all. The teacher tried to go on with the lesson.

Soon the teacher began to see and hear some snickers and smiles spread across the faces of some of the students before him. He was not able to figure out what the issue was and after continuing on with the lesson further there came a point in time when his eyes met those of a student who couldn't take the disruption anymore. That student nodded his head toward the light switch, tipping the teacher off to what Mike was doing. When the teacher looked over, there was Mike facing the light switch with his back to the teacher and to the rest of the class.

He was holding both of his middle fingers up while facing the light switch. The teacher had not noticed that the lights never went off when he asked Mike to flick them off. The teacher angrily asked Mike what he was doing. As Mike turned around to answer the teacher, he was now holding both of his middle fingers up toward the teacher. "You asked me to flick off the lights," was Mike's simple response.

In that one moment in time, it would have been very easy for the teacher to bring the hammer down on Mike because of the kind of student he was. But the teacher could tell by the look in Mike's eyes that what he did was exactly what he thought the teacher had asked him to do. There was no malice and no disrespect, though it would have been easy for the teacher to interpret the situation in that way. It was just the reality Mike lived in at the time. Needless to say, the teacher learned very quickly to ask, "Will you please turn the lights off?" instead of "Will you please flick the lights off?"

In the second year of teaching, Mr. Sanders, an eighth-grade teacher in Nebraska, witnessed something happen on the first day of school that he would never forget. Against his better judgment, he went along with the typical process of getting all of the junior high students in one room and discussing the rules with them for two hours. Actually, *reading* the rules out of the parent handbook would be a better way to describe it. He immediately recognized that reading the rules out loud would insult anyone's intelligence, including eighth-grade students.

Anyway, the idea was that each teacher would address a particular area. During this wonderful intellectual exchange of meaningful thoughts and ideas about learning, another eighth-grade teacher was reading over the rule that stated that students weren't allowed to chew gum or drink soda pop during class. As this teacher was reading the rules to students, she was also sitting on her desk, chewing gum, and drinking coffee from a thermos during the entire monologue.

Like most other principals, this one would give tours of the building from time to time to prospective parents. The principal had set up one of these tours with a set of parents to take place approximately one hour after school got out. It was after the teacher-contracted hours. The parents wanted to see the entire building, but they really wanted to see the fifth-grade classrooms as their daughter would be in the fifth grade. At the time the principal felt like he had three very good fifth-grade teachers, but one that was exceptional. And the parents were very impressed with the entire building until they came to this exceptional teacher's classroom.

This exceptional teacher was not exceptional at organization. When the principal turned the lights on, he could audibly hear a gasp from the mouths of both parents when they saw the teacher's desk. Every principal and every other professional leader worth their salt out there will tell you that organization is not always an indicator of teaching ability. Lack of organizational skills does not always equate to lack of teaching skills. The outside world, however, does not always see it that way.

This set of parents did not see it that way. From that point forward nothing the principal could say was going to change the minds of the parents regarding their thoughts about this particular teacher's teaching ability. The parents also made it clear that the fact that the principal would even try to defend the teacher made him look like he didn't know what he was talking about either. And the principal never saw those parents again. Some might argue this as a problem, others as a blessing. It depends on how you view the situation. A similar concept regarding perception will come up again in chapter 9 when we discuss the one-hundred-yard rule. But one thing at a time.

THE THEORY

In almost all cases, and certainly in these three stories, perception is much more powerful than reality. In most cases, perception cements reality in the mind of a noneducator when judging the actions of a professional leader in education. That's just the way it is sometimes. This is a critical thing to remember regardless of your position in the field of education. In education, we have a bad habit of underestimating the general public when it comes to how they perceive us. What the preceding three stories all have in common exemplifies the importance of professional leaders in understanding the fundamental difference between perception and reality.

For Mike's fellow classmates that day, they all thought that Mike had done this on purpose just to be funny because he was the class clown. The teacher showed veteran savvy in handling it correctly.

However, because the teacher never corrected Mike's classmates about this perception, the teacher fed into a vicious circle of learned helplessness on Mike's part. Mike learned that regardless of mistakes that he made, as long as he acted as if it were a joke, no one could judge him based on his intelligence or his academic achievement. It became his defense mechanism.

Mike also taught his teacher a very tough but important lesson that year not only about perception, but about the importance of correcting perception where it is incorrect. Rarely would a professional leader in education get the same opportunity in the outside world. In this case, as the adult and as the teacher, that person was the only one that knew Mike was not joking and that he thought he was only doing what the teacher had asked him to. While showing veteran poise in correcting perception with Mike, it may have been helpful to take it a step further and correct it with the rest of the class as well.

In the second story the message is clear. Never assume that because you are an adult and a professional leader, especially in education, that you are better than someone else or should have more privileges or rights than someone else, including your students. The rules still do apply to you as the adult and as the professional leader. We preach in education the modeling of teaching what we expect from our students during lessons. Yet we sometimes forget that valuable lesson when it comes to following those same rules as professional leaders and as adults.

Taking this one step further, I would be willing to bet that our higher education colleagues, if truly being honest, would tell us that it is the teachers in their classes that make the worst students at the graduate level. Oftentimes I have sat in on classes full of mostly teachers in which they mirror the behaviors of their own students by participating in side conversations during class, negotiating assignments, turning in sloppy work, and so on. Sometimes as professional leaders and as adults we do not model as students what we might expect of our own students.

The third story teaches us that no matter how good we may be at our jobs, in education, it is equally as important to make it look good as well. Every little thing we do in education is being evaluated sometimes by those outside of education. Perception becomes critical when you are always working in a fishbowl environment. Even though we are now in the twenty-first century, most citizens in our communities may still have a 1950s mindset when they think about the professional leaders teaching their children.

This is where common sense really applies and the following message is not rocket science; it is simply stating again what should be the obvious. This means most citizens don't really want to see you as a professional leader sitting on the bar stool next to them. They don't want to see you speeding past them on the road when they have their kids in the car. They don't want to see you breaking the rules. As archaic as this may seem, these expectations do still come with the job to some degree whether we like it or not and even though it doesn't exist in our contracts.

THE PRACTICE

As administrators and as teachers, common sense should tell you that you as a professional leader must always be wary of how you come across to the public. In our society, we like to think we have come a long way in terms of how we view people and each other. This isn't necessarily the case with education, even though it is the one field that should be further along with this concept than any other. Parents still want their children's teacher to be the old school, straight-laced, upstanding citizen that is a role model in all areas of life, public and private. Some think it would be cool if you were sitting on a bar stool next to them but will raise a riot if it ever actually happens. Some think it would be really neat if you e-mailed their child through Facebook, but will call the authorities when it really happens. A good rule of thumb: if there is any apprehension or just a gut feeling that something isn't right in your actions, or in what someone else is asking you to do, follow your instinct. It's tough to go wrong following that advice.

If you work in a school, don't do things like drive a fancy or expensive car to work. This isn't a status symbol in education like it might be in the business world. There are still parents who might view this as rubbing it in that you think you are better than they are, that you are making more money than they are, that you have a better job with benefits than they do, and so on. Yes, I know it's crazy. But remember it's perception that is important here, not reality. If you have the resources to own a fancy car, I have two things for you. The first is that I wish I were you. The second is that you might want to consider driving it on the weekends and before and after school, just not to school. Yes, it is widely acknowledged that most professional leaders in education are grossly underpaid, but there are still parents out there that think otherwise and you probably know that already.

All this talk about perception should make you realize that sometimes you have to fake it, act it, whatever you want to call it. If organization isn't your strength, fake it. At least put things into piles when you leave at the end of the day. It is very unlikely that an observer would have any idea that it is a completely unorganized pile. If you have a student that legitimately has a perception that it is okay to flick off the lights, correct it with both the student and the class. If you want to drink coffee and chew gum even when your students aren't allowed to, hide it. Do it in the lounge or out of sight of students. And as you go about your business in the community, have fun and do your own thing. But be careful not to give parents, other citizens, and the rest of the outside world any more ammunition than they may already have in not understanding how education works.

Yes, all this perception stuff is common sense, but what do perception and reality have to do with school change? The same point is going to be made here that you will read about again in chapter 9. When you are ready to implement school change, chances are good you are going to need as many people as possible outside of your four walls on your side. This includes those outsiders who live both in and out of your district. We want people outside of our buildings to be on our side when we are ready to implement school change because sometimes it is those people that control where the money goes, what the curriculum is, what the priorities are, and so on. I didn't say it was right, but that's how it is sometimes and I have a hunch you may already know that as well.

It seems simple, right? Seems like common sense, right? So you are now more than halfway through the text of this highly stimulating work. Surely you have questions?

CHAPTER 8

What Questions Do You Have?

THE STORY

Have you asked yourself why professional leaders find it necessary to ask the group of people in front of them, whether it be adults, individual students, or a class as a whole after instruction, "Are there any questions?" This makes little sense to me and it happens all the time, sometimes with seasoned presenters. In working with teachers, a principal once advised the teachers not to do this and some still did because the principal never told them why it wasn't good practice. For any professional leader who may read this book and has asked that question in that manner I would urge you to change your line of questioning.

If you are a professional leader talking with adults and you really want to know the answer to this question, you will never truly get it. So why not? For the same reason that your students won't raise their hands when the question is asked in this manner. Because by asking this question in this way, you are putting the person or group of people in front of you in a no-win situation. What you are really telling them is this: if you are a dummy and weren't paying attention, now is the time to ask a question that I already answered once. The nature of the question itself suggests that you expect there not to be any questions. If it is in a classroom and a student really does have a question, especially if shy, he or she will never ask it under these circumstances and here's the reason why. Big news flash: he or she will be embarrassed. And the same holds true sometimes for adults in those situations.

When the professional leader asks the question in that way, it assumes that the person in front of them should have understood the directions in the first place. The sheer nature of the question assumes that no one would possibly be dumb enough to not understand the directions or the instructions you just gave. The question itself makes the assumption that there shouldn't be any questions. In the off chance an adult or a student is brave enough to ask a question, they must do so when every other adult or student in the group may already know the answer and is now looking at them. So how do the really good professional leaders get around this?

Subtly turning around the verbiage in the question makes all difference in the world. "What questions do you have?" This question now tells the adults in a meeting or the students in the class that you as the professional leader will expect someone to have questions. Heck, you might be expecting everyone to have a question now. Any professional leader who can get into the habit of making this simple change in questioning will realize that by creating a risk-free environment in which questions are expected, you are also creating a higher likelihood that you will get the honest questions in response to your instruction that you were really hoping for. It's not just about changing the question, it's about creating a risk-free environment that encourages and expects questioning both from students and from other professional leaders.

THE THEORY

Recognize the moments and recognize the ability level of those around you. In the educational field, most professional leaders look for and revel in what are called "teachable moments." These are rare times when an unplanned situation arises in which a professional leader has an opportunity to capitalize on teaching an adult or a student or a group of students in a way that may never be replicated again. This is a magical moment in time for any professional leader and an incredible learning experience for the professional leader and the student, regardless of age. The professional leader feels it and knows it, sometimes by instinct alone.

Think of the possibilities if we could capture and capitalize on that magical moment and apply it to other important moments in education, like recognizing immediately that an embarrassed student or professional leader doesn't know the answer and providing a risk-free way to divert attention and still encourage the student or the professional leader to participate. If we could find a way to realize that there are adults that are uncomfortable in a discussion because of the content, we could change the path of the discussion without a feeling of awkwardness. Think of the great things that could be accomplished in education if we were all capable of recognizing the moments to the same degree consistently. Think of the trust and caring that could be established.

Think of the possibilities if we were able to look inside the minds of other professionals in education and clearly see what their true capabilities were. There is a fine line between pushing professionals out of their comfort zone in order to have them grow personally and professionally and forcing someone to do something they are truly uncomfortable with because they acknowledge that they are just not capable of what is being asked. The second scenario usually creates irreparable damage to the relationship of the asker and the askee. Again, if it were possible, if it could be done, think of the trust and caring that could be established.

THE PRACTICE

You may be asking yourself, what does proper question asking have to do with successful school change? Again, it isn't about the question asking; it is about creating the right environment for successful school change to take place. Besides what was already covered in chapter 7, successful school change often hinges on how we perceive problem solving and the people around us. If that is an understood notion, then the hard part becomes: How do we recognize the moments? How do we recognize the ability level of those around us when it is not clearly visible? Here, there are some commonsense ground rules to go over.

First and foremost, when you recognize a moment, never announce it. The moment is then gone. Simply have the flexibility to recognize it inwardly and act on it outwardly without the verbalization. Moments are both easy and impossible to recognize all at the same time, but both involve your own ability to read people's faces, gestures, movements, vocal tone, and so on. Sometimes it involves making a judgment call about the importance of an action.

In gauging the ability levels of other professional leaders and students, there are more general rules. If you are a professional leader, never argue with an individual in front of a group. This means that a board member does not argue with an administrator at a public board meeting. This means that administrators do not argue with a teacher at a staff meeting. It means that teachers do not argue with a student in front of a class, and so on.

This simply cannot happen because it allows the breakdown of the very structure that successful education is based upon. There are always lines that should be walked up to and flirted with but also those that should not be crossed or even ventured toward. Present to your students or to your staff unique ways of problem solving for solutions, but make sure that arguing isn't one of them. When you argue in front of a crowd, you are acknowledging that it is okay with you that there is not order when you are around.

Understand that the argument with that person may still be necessary, but should take place in a different environment that does not involve the rest of the group watching and judging. This keeps order and everyone's dignity intact. This is an important step because all successful school change requires input, both positive and negative. But all input must have order or the change you so desire will never stand the test of time, no matter how successful it may seem initially.

Here is a golden rule and a commonsense rule to remember as you go forward with change: As a professional leader, never ask another to do something that you wouldn't do yourself. It is a critical element to consider for successful school change to take place on any level.

Too often we find ourselves caught up in the game of reprimand. Consequences. Punishments. Whatever term it is that your district calls it. While there is clearly a time and a place for that, we often do not accurately perceive the time or the place. When something goes wrong, it is human nature to either avoid confrontation altogether or to want to immediately find the source of the problem and to systematically deal with it. For those of us that want to deal with it immediately, there are some things to consider. The first rule that should apply before any action is taken is the same one that will be discussed further in chapter

11. Is it a situation that requires immediate attention or is it a situation where you should let the problem ripen? Whether you are dealing with adults or children, the second question that professional leaders should ask themselves is this: Are we trying to catch them, or are we trying to help them? Whether dealing with adults or children, ask yourself that question again and be very careful about what the answer may be and about what you think the answer should be.

Whether you are dealing with disciplinary action for adults or for children, you don't always have to follow the rules. You don't always have to follow the district policy. There are times when it is okay to lose a policy battle in order to win a public opinion battle. There are times when it is okay to lose the public opinion battle in order to win the policy battle. The rub is whether or not you as a successful professional leader can recognize which is which. This ability might also be helpful in promoting change in your district, whether with students or with professional leaders.

Here is an example of what I mean. Let's say that Johnny and Sally did not turn in their assignment one day in class. Johnny is a role model student and a role model citizen that other students look up to. Johnny is an intelligent, respectful, polite student that has never had a detention in his entire academic career. Johnny did the assignment and legitimately forgot it at home that day. This was due to an unfortunate circumstance that happened at his home that morning that distracted him.

Let's say that Sally is a student that is constantly in trouble and is about to set the world record for the amount of detentions received in an academic year. I'm sure you do not have any Sallies at your school, but for the sake of argument, let's just say that like Johnny, Sally is very intelligent, but she does different things. Sally enjoys talking back to teachers, disrupting classes, antagonizing other students and has a long history of missing assignments even though she is very capable and has had sufficient time to do them.

The rule or the policy states that the teacher should be issuing both students a detention because they were both not done with their assignment. This is a situation where it is okay to lose the policy battle in order to win the public opinion battle. As stated in chapter 2, what is fair for one doesn't necessarily mean it is fair for all. As a district, ask yourselves when dealing with these types of situations, will it be your district philosophy that you are trying to catch kids or are you trying to help kids? As a district, it is beneficial to send the message to your community that you believe in giving a break to the students who have done the right thing most of the time, regardless of what your district or school policy may say. It is okay to come down more harshly on a student that is purposely defying the rule simply for his or her own enjoyment and has done so repeatedly.

This is okay so long as you remember that just because Sally has cheated before, this doesn't mean she is guilty. There has to be proof as basis for decision making here. Past regressions should not lead professional leaders to assume that a person's negative record, student or adult, equates to guilt.

Sally's parents will undoubtedly ask the question: What did you do about Johnny? Or, Why didn't Johnny get the same punishment as Sally? The first question should be handled as it would be in chapter 2. I will discuss your child with you, but I will not discuss someone else's child with you. The second question is where you lose the policy battle to win the public opinion battle. When Sally's parent appeals, the outcome will not matter. The district has already won the public opinion battle. They have done the morally correct thing.

A teacher breaks up a fight. In the course of doing so, he must use restraint against a student to prevent the possibility of jeopardizing the safety of either an adult or a student. The community views it as excessive force and wishes for the administration and/or the board to have something done to the teacher. The administration has a choice. Even though the professional leader did the right thing and likely prevented others from getting hurt, they could take action to appease the community. If they follow their own policy, they can back the professional leader 100 percent and issue a statement of support and commendation. And here, they had better do so.

Again the district should think about the message they want their administration to send to the community and to their professional leaders. Is it okay to give in to the community and throw a professional leader who did the right thing under the bus simply to avoid a large-scale confrontation with the community? Is it okay to promote the jeopardizing of another adult or student safety through nonaction simply to avoid a public outcry? Here is a situation where it is okay to lose the public opinion battle in order to win the policy battle.

Priorities, priorities. Right is right and in education, education is not first. Safety is always first, education second, and a lot of other things third. Regardless of whether it is a public opinion battle or a policy battle, recognize the situation for what it is and use common sense to act accordingly. The beginning of this chapter started with a simple question. Now I have another for you. Though it may be called something else in your part of the country, have you ever heard of the one-hundred-yard rule?

CHAPTER 9

The One-Hundred-Yard Rule

THE STORY

A former administrator in Milwaukee explained this rule to me once a long time ago and it stuck and I have no idea why or how. I thought I had forgotten about it altogether until I was putting ideas together for this book. It may seem silly at first, but I think you will agree by the end of the chapter that it makes sense. It goes something like this. A stranger pulls into the parking lot at your school. Maybe she is there for a meeting. Maybe she is a new parent wanting to tour the school to see if she would like her child to attend there. Maybe it is a public official who wants to visit the school as part of public relations for the upcoming election. Maybe it is the auditor who has arrived to conduct an audit. Regardless of who she is, pretend for the sake of argument as if she has never been to your school before.

Let's say the person parks in the lot, gets out of the vehicle, and looks around. Ask yourself, What does she see? Is it a highly manicured campus with no debris? Is it a parking lot with lots of potholes and garbage stuck in the playground fence? Would she see a highly maintained building on the exterior that is crisp and clean? Or would she see the mortar is crumbling and there are cracks in the windows?

It is once the person gets out of the car and begins the walk to the door of your district's building where the fun begins. Once people get within one hundred yards of the door to your building, their minds are made up about your building, inside and out. That's right. You have read that right. They have already made up their minds about your school before they have walked in the door.

They already have a preconceived notion about your school and they are about to create another preconceived notion about the employees inside your school the second they walk through the door. They already have created an opinion about your students and their parents. They already have ideas about the community. And on and on. And here is the kicker. As weird as it may sound, there is a significant amount of truth to the One-Hundred-Yard Rule. Reversing the first impression of outsiders is next to impossible. It means that the outsiders have made up their minds about your school without seeing the inside. They have made up their minds about your staff maybe without talking with anyone. And based on those two things they may have made assumptions about your community and the citizens that reside there. The lesson here is that it is pretty important that you get it right on the exterior and on the interior the first time around. If you want to facilitate change, sometimes you need all of these people on your side for it to happen successfully.

THE THEORY

The one-hundred-yard rule in theory means that we have to think ahead of time about the impression we leave on those outside of education. My ex-military wife (not my ex-wife, my ex-military wife) would apply the six Ps theory here that she learned in the Army: Prior Planning Prevents Piss Poor Performance. Applied to our field, this means professional leaders always have to think before they act, before they make decisions, before they speak at public meetings.

This is because there is still a segment of society that holds professional leaders up to a higher standard, as discussed in chapter 7. Though professional leaders should take that as a compliment, they should also be careful to always phrase meaning in general terms, knowing that doing so commits them to nothing and leaves them with multiple options for problem solving later. This is a critical step not just to creating successful school change, but to sustaining it over time.

So the theory here becomes simple. Try to make it look good even when it is not good. Make it sound good even when it does not sound good. Some call this smoke and mirrors and it isn't always easy to do.

But creating successful school change and being able to sustain it over time requires buy-in from more than just the district staff. Sometimes it involves parts or all of the community and other outsiders as well. So be sure to brag publicly and complain privately and make sure every other professional leader in your district believes this, does this, and understands why this theory in practice is so important to the long-term success of the district, whether trying to be a part of successful school change or not.

THE PRACTICE

People talk. The reality is that it doesn't matter how big or small your district is, people talk and they are talking about you. That has been true since the days of the one-room schoolhouse and will probably never change. The key here is channeling the chatter in the direction the district wants it to go. You want to get the chatter moving in the right direction because it is easy to shake a good reputation but very difficult to shake a bad one. Not impossible, but difficult. Sustaining successful school change is many parts of a whole. That you already knew without reading this book. It is common sense. Sustaining successful school change is partially about the talk in and outside of your district being in your favor. People move to your community based on this talk. They send their children to your school as a result of this talk. They donate their time, services, and money because of this talk. Most importantly, they will support the change that schools want to make when the time is right because of the talk.

A very good principal in an urban school once told me that she didn't believe in the one-hundred-yard rule. She didn't believe that talk could change anything in the inner city. I challenged her to let me have the chance to prove her wrong. Through coaxing, she was able to secure a small amount of funds. With a minor amount of arm twisting, she was able to get a very small amount of volunteers. Through communication from teachers to parents, she was able to get certain things or services donated, like a lawn mower every other weekend. Like a seventy-five-year-old retired steel worker who loved gardening and who loved volunteering his time and money to do so at the school.

With the help of her custodians, some continued challenges and motivation, and some serious organization on her part, she was able to completely transform her campus in two months. It was no longer called the school grounds. It was called the school campus. The lawn was treated, cared for, and mowed every other weekend for free. Flower beds were planted, weeded, and maintained for free. Different parts of the inside and of the outside of the building were painted for free on a rotating basis. The garbage was picked up in shifts for free throughout the school year. Word got out and volunteers began lining up, parents and senior citizens alike. Over time and in the middle of the inner city, they created a gem.

After three summers of this, her school was crawling with a combination of the highest-caliber students and students that wanted to be the highest caliber of students. There was a long waiting list to get into her school. Volunteers who wanted to help inside and outside all year at times had to be turned away. After the first summer of this, what was happening on the inside of the building began to change as well in interesting ways. The attitude of the students, the teachers, and the parents began to change.

After two years of this, her staff of professional leaders were ready for the hardest part, real school change—change related to instruction, curriculum, evaluation, and professional development. The community was ready to support any initiative that the principal was ready to propose. To date, the school remains a sea of tranquility in the middle of one of the biggest storms of a city in America. A wonderful, free-spirited professional leader and a strong and stubborn principal, she is surrounded by those who now spend a significant amount of time listening instead of critiquing and learning the commonsense lessons in how she did it.

All districts, no matter how big or small, should devote a certain amount of money to building and grounds maintenance. This should be done specifically as a result of the one-hundred-yard rule. Though it should be no secret to superintendents and school boards, not all of them do it. In times of economic crisis, it only takes a bare minimum amount of money and people to volunteer to change an image. At times, it only requires enough money to buy paint, make sure the lawn is mowed, those types of things. Doing this will go a long way toward getting the right chatter going about your district.

If you as a professional school leader want to start making meaningful school change that will sustain itself over time, common sense should tell you that there is something to be said for starting with the acknowledgment of the one-hundred-yard rule. Take the free lessons that it offers and make them your own.

If you can master the one-hundred-yard rule and make it your own, you will get parents involved. Getting parents involved *changes* schools. Have you noticed how often a word is used in italics in this book? This is one of the few times it has been done. That is how important this sentence is. I will repeat it for emphasis. Getting parents involved *changes* schools. No matter where the school is, whether in the inner city of Detroit or in the very smallest school district in Idaho. Earlier I said I would use very few references outside of chapter 5. But trust me when I tell you that if you are interested, there is an incredible amount of research out there that proves that if you can master the one-hundred-yard rule and if you create parent involvement as a result, successful school change happens simply by default.

So it is crucial that your approach to the one-hundred-yard rule is dead on. Do it right and do it right the first time. Make it a focus and a priority, not just to implement successful school change, but to sustain it. Don't forget about it after the honeymoon period, either. Forgetting about it after the honeymoon can only begin the process of getting caught in the trap of success discussed in chapter 1. Forgetting how you started is where a lot of districts take a step back. If you have been interested in the advice in this book so far and paying a little bit of attention, you know that rolling out change occurs at the right time and after the right groundwork discussed up to this point has been laid.

This groundwork includes things like understanding the dangers of the trap of success before you begin implementing school change, not worrying about things you cannot control like what you may perceive as being fair or not fair, getting the right fit, getting everyone on the same train and moving in the same direction, CARING, knowing that money solves nothing when it comes to school change, the importance of understanding the differences between perception and reality and how that affects your ability to create school change, and knowing the kinds of messages you want to send to your community not only about school change, but about how you do business in general.

At this point, mastering the one-hundred-yard rule should just seem like plain common sense and you are having a "duh" moment because you cannot believe you have read this to be reminded of how simple things can be. And hopefully you realize it can be so easy to do and can cost just about nothing. Now let's talk about trust and the long division story and how it can help to establish trust further and how that trust can further help to facilitate successful and sustained school change.

CHAPTER 10

Long Division

THE STORY

Some time ago, I was talking with a teacher about an issue in her district regarding the math curriculum. The district, eight years prior, had switched math programs and adopted a new math curriculum. At the time, they took an incredible amount of flack from community residents. In addition, teachers were not sold on the reverse spiraling aspect of the curriculum. As a compromise the superintendent told residents that teachers would still be allowed to "supplement" the curriculum with standard skill and drill activities. Eight years later, the district was still having poor results on their state standardized test scores in math. Our discussion revolved around why that might still be occurring.

In the course of our discussion, the subject of long division came up. The teacher explained to me that as a fifth-grade teacher, she felt it critical that students be capable of long division in order to be successful in sixth-grade math. She felt her students came to her at the beginning of the year severely lacking in this area. As a result, she took about a month spending time on a skill and drill unit specifically designed to improve long division skills.

I asked her what unit or lessons that were originally slated for that time did she skip in order to spend another month on long division. After telling me that she picked an area she felt her students were strong in, I began to think maybe a pattern was possible in this district. I asked if she thought other teachers who taught in lower grades had a similar mindset about the math curriculum and how to go about supplementing it. She was certain that they did.

So I began to play out the following scenario for her. What if the first-grade teachers thought a particular math concept was critically important in order to prepare their students for success in the second grade? As a result the first-grade teachers agreed to spend a month using a unit specifically designed to improve that skill. However, in the process of doing so, they just so happened to skip the section in the math book that set the groundwork for learning long division because students at that time seemed to have mastered it. And let's say the second-grade teachers did the exact same thing, and happened to skip the section on long division. Let's say the third-grade teachers happened to also repeat the same process. Could this be the explanation for why the fifth-grade students do not know how to do long division when they enter the fifth grade?

THE THEORY

There is a premise in Daniel Johnson's (2005) book *Sustaining Change in Schools* that if you ask quality questions, you will get the honest answers about school change that you may be seeking. Trouble is, if there is not a trust factor involved or if there is a fear of retribution for honesty, whether real or perceived, all of the quality questions you've developed won't mean much. There has to be a trust established if you want to get the real answers you are looking for.

All great relationships are based on trust. It doesn't matter if they are personal or professional; they are all based on trust. In the scenario played out here there is a fundamental lack of trust among the professional leaders in this district. Integrity is everywhere but trust is not. Integrity might be easily identifiable everywhere in the building or it might be a real struggle to find it within an entire district, depending on where you look. But integrity is there somewhere to some degree, which is different from trust. Even in the best schools, sometimes trust is missing altogether and it's possible an explanation is necessary as to why this is a problem outside of the obvious.

In the long division story all of the professional leaders involved think they have the students' best interests in mind. And it is clear that they do. However, it may be that over the course of time some of them have lost a clear view of the bigger picture of what is best for their students. It is possible that the four walls of the classroom they teach in have clouded what they see outside of the classroom, which has had an impact on their trust in the math curriculum and in other professional leaders around them. Their integrity, however, cannot be questioned. Like most professional leaders in education, their integrity level is incredible.

In this story it is the trust that is lacking and this is a commonality that is way too frequent in education. We don't always trust the system, even in our own systems in our own districts. We trust ourselves. We don't always trust that the job is being done by our fellow teachers, administrators, or even school boards. We don't always trust the curriculum, especially if it is new. We don't trust that it will cover what we think is essential and important. What common sense should tell you is that sometimes trust should be more common.

We are professionals, for crying out loud. And every one of us was hired for a reason. And probably a damn good one. To fill a role or a niche that was missing. To provide a talent or a strength that was missing. Likewise, curriculums are generally adopted for a lot of the same reasons. Trust that professional leaders working with you will do the job they were hired to do. Trust that the curriculum you are using has a reason for its existence in your district. Whether or not you agree with it will not change that fact.

One character trait that professional leaders have to possess in order for successful change in schools to grow and develop is the ability to separate. Think about this the next time you are sitting in a staff meeting. The professional leader in your building that you believe is the most incompetent leader is giving a workshop in front of you and the rest of the staff. Are you capable of setting aside your personal feelings about the speaker or about the content of the speech in order to truly listen and to learn from what they are saying?

This is a character trait that not a lot of professionals possess, including those in education, and including myself at different times, I am sorry to say. Professional leaders must continue to develop their ability to listen to the message. This should be a career-long endeavor. Regardless of your role in education, this may be the single most important trait for you to continue to develop for any real change to happen, whether that be for your own professional growth or for your district in the long term. We will talk about how you can develop this trait further in the "Practice" section.

When teaching a new curriculum, set aside the fact that you may not agree with the curriculum. Actually try teaching the curriculum as it was presented. Trust that there is meaning to doing so. You may find that you too will find meaning in your own teaching by doing so. Being a follower isn't a trait that professional leaders brag about possessing. Even though some of the very best professional leaders in education are followers, it is correctly argued that following blindly is not healthy in education.

However, a little bit of blind faith does not always hurt, either. Common sense alone should tell you that everything is in place, whether it be people or curriculum, for a reason. Though it is good and healthy to question, we must also remember that sometimes we have to understand that it is not always our place to know what that reason is. And if professional leaders can understand that concept, it can guide them to knowing the appropriate time and place both for questioning and for following direction. This knowledge can also help to guide professional leaders in understanding the importance of establishing trust as it relates to school change.

Professional leaders have to trust in the powers above them that they have put the right people in the right position to be successful and for students to be successful. You don't have to like them and you don't have to always agree with them. But professional leaders also have to trust that if someone is not pulling their weight, whoever is responsible for taking care of it is working on it already, including between the administration and the board and between the board and the citizens of the community.

THE PRACTICE

Professional leaders do not need to create their own integrity; 99 percent of those in education have already clearly established integrity that will never be questioned. They may, however, need to be able to create their own trust. We alone have control of our own trust. This comes as no surprise to any of us. It cannot be taught to us and it cannot be forced upon us. And if we are going to trust, do not fake it. I have suggested faking it at a couple of different points in this book. Faking it is definitely not appropriate when it comes to trust.

When it comes to trust, if it is not genuine, if it is not a genuine effort that is sincere, it is not worth the effort. If we in education are going to stand up for what is best for kids, we must force ourselves to be objective enough to see the bigger picture of what is best for our students. When it comes to trust, professional leaders should not be inhibited by the four walls of their own classroom or the four walls of their own office or by the four walls of their own minds.

Sometimes when it comes to trust, applying some common sense is much more difficult than it needs to be. Remember, we are not working in the business world, as much as some outsiders would like us to be. Distrust can be an advantage in some areas in business, in politics, and in the rest of the world. However, there is never an advantage to distrust in the field of education. Sometimes there are things from the business world that are applicable in schools, but trust is an area where the two fields can split drastically.

To trust in others, as in any field, professional leaders in education must first be able to listen. Here's a simple question that isn't always so simple when you watch professional colleagues in education interact with each other: How do we listen? A professional leader from Idaho was telling me that she struggled while listening to others because she spent the entire duration of the discussion thinking about what else she needed to do, others she needed to talk to, and so on. Outwardly, she knew she was hiding it well, but inwardly was becoming frustrated with her own patience. And I can tell you that as well as you think you may be hiding it, others are probably still picking up on the fact that you are checked out. Most professional leaders in education can relate to this. So again the question is asked: How do we listen?

What divides us in education takes a long time of practicing to fix. Hence the title of this chapter: Long Division. To listen takes patience, which takes time, but most of all, it takes objectivity. The issue isn't applying objectivity to the discussions with those we respect because that is easy. The issue is applying objectivity to the discussions with those we do not respect. Professional leaders cannot properly listen until they master this skill first. All of these things establish trust.

Professional leaders in education usually have the potential to learn the most from those that they believe have the least potential to teach them. That is why it is a struggle to listen with objectivity. But the biggest and most important changes in education cannot occur without this process taking place. Patience, patience, patience and trust, trust, trust. Inwardly and outwardly. Let me say one thing to school boards out there. The establishment of trust starts at the top. If you have tried and tried and still cannot find it within you to succeed at this, there is another option. Let the problem ripen. . . .

CHAPTER 11

Let the Problem Ripen

THE STORY

Like many great educators, Dr. Sorenson has been a fountain of knowledge without ever knowing it. Now a professor at the doctoral level, he enlightens every day not only students that he teaches, but anytime he interacts with others. During one of his classes, a professional leader that was also a student had spent a considerable amount of time complaining about the various issues in the district he worked for. The professional leader went on and on discussing how he could solve all the problems of the district and in the world in general, if only he were the superintendent.

Dr. Sorenson posed a question to this professional leader: "What is the hurry?" The professional leader and the entire class of professional leaders were staggered by the question and left wondering what the answer was to such a simple yet profound question. The professional leader asked for some clarification. "Sometimes as a professional leader, it is best to let the problem ripen," Dr. Sorenson said. This flabbergasted the professional leader to the point that he did not know what to say in response. Eventually the professional leader gathered his wits and worked up the courage to ask Dr. Sorenson what he really meant by that.

Since then the students from Dr. Sorenson's classes have spent a lot of time explaining to their own professional leaders the same thing that Dr. Sorenson explained to them. It is not necessary and can sometimes be detrimental to be in such a hurry to immediately correct every problem that exists. It doesn't make you look any better and doesn't mean you are more effective simply because you were more timely.

In fact, the opposite is usually true. It is in our rush to solve problems that we make the biggest mistakes, which usually ends up contributing to the problem instead of solving it. Professional leaders, both in the classroom and in the office, can get themselves into hot water by rushing to judgment. Let the problem ripen. Keep in mind that most of the problems that professional leaders think need to be solved immediately are the ones that come up either during the implementation of change or during the process of the change itself. It is then that the idea to let it ripen should come back to you.

THE THEORY

Ninety percent of the decisions we make in education do not need to be made immediately and will find a solution themselves without intervention if we let the problem ripen. The disclaimer here is to be very cognizant of the fact that there is also a very fine line between letting a problem ripen and letting it rot. Always know where that line is. Sometimes professional leaders with quick decision making habits not only make mistakes in their decisions, but allow that habit to actually inhibit their potential to be great. This can kill successful school change. That is Dr. Sorenson's lesson.

In explaining further the theory of letting the problem ripen, there are several reasons why it may be important that professional leaders consider adopting this mantra not for all decision making, but certainly for the times and the situations when it is appropriate during the school change process. The field of education is unique in that there are times that arise in a classroom or in a school when a professional leader may actually want a problem to get worse before they go about trying to solve it. It may be to prove a point to a person or a student or a group of people or a classroom of students. You may want other people to discuss the matter to bring the problem to a head. You may want others to solve it for you.

The problem that can exist in education (and possibly in other fields as well) is that it is human nature of good professional leaders to want to take care of problems as soon as they happen. The mistake that occurs in doing so is that we eliminate the possibility for reflection while the problem is ripening. It eliminates the possibility of learning about others and their problem solving skills under pressure. Immediate decision making when it is not necessary does not facilitate successful school change.

Learning about how others go about solving problems or dealing with adversity are all things that are helpful to know about professional leaders and students when implementing school change. It is this type of theory that helps professional leaders know what to expect from professional leaders during initial stages of school change. Applying the logic of "let the problem ripen" to educational situations also allows for the possibility of the elimination of emotion in critical decision making. However, it is important to remember that this is not a theory to be used universally, but rather to apply appropriately. Many situations in education are ones where decisions must be made immediately, but if you've been around a while it is pretty easy to tell the difference between the two. You don't need me to tell you that.

THE PRACTICE

Like many other theories, this theory in practice may create some problems along the way. That is something you can probably count on because of the sheer nature of the idea. However, this is not always a bad thing. In fact, it is the very nature of the theory to promote the problem. To steal a line from Paul Romer (Friedman, 2005) used in Michael Fullan's (2008) work *The Six Secrets of Change*: "A crisis is a terrible thing to waste!" Successful school change that stands the test of time cannot be done in a hurry, either in decision making or in process. Common sense tells us that.

Though it sounds great and easy, in practice there are at least two important elements to keep in mind using the "let it ripen" theory of problem solving. The first is that it will require patience and the second is the commonsense part. And that is that it should not be applied universally. Patience, patience, patience and trust, trust, trust. Notice this is the second chapter where the word patience used. It is a critical element not only for application of this theory, but for any successful school change.

In order to be successful and patient in applying this theory, you must be confident and have trust in your own ability as an administrator or as a teacher, and in the ability of those around you. Professional leaders who are newer to the field oftentimes will struggle with this concept, usually as a result of a lack of experience or a lack of confidence in their own abilities. And it makes sense that a lack of experience might sometimes lead to a lack of confidence. Professional leaders have to be capable of trusting in themselves and knowing they are doing the right thing when letting the problem ripen. This is one of many things in education that are sometimes easier said than done.

The second limitation to the theory is that it must be gauged and applied to different situations differently. Professional leaders should never allow a problem to ripen in a situation where it can be permanently damaging to other people, especially students, or to the district. Remember that there are also situations where you will have to recognize that the process you choose could be damaging to you or permanently damaging to your reputation. It also would not make sense to apply this theory in emergency type situations where it is critical that decisions are made quickly.

So what does this theory have to do with school change? The theory should be applied differently during various stages of school change. During the initial stages of school change implementation, it is probably wise to use this theory sparingly. This is not the time to keep people waiting. During the middle stages of implementation, however, and after change has been established, is a different story. So the further along you are in your school change process, the more liberally this theory can be applied, which should really make some sense when you think about it.

Many times the letting the problem ripen theory is an effective strategy to use in a mentoring situation with students or other professional leaders or as opportunities to use the theory itself as a professional development tool. Another layer of the "let it ripen" theory involves the concept of baiting. This is much like going fishing. The idea here is when it comes time for intervention on the part of the professional leader to make a decision, the professional leader prolongs the decision one last time and instead applies the baiting theory.

This means that you throw out several alternate solutions, much like trying various lures in fishing, knowing all along that one of them is probably the correct one. The purpose for doing this is twofold. The first is to see if you can provide one more last chance for whoever is involved in the problem solving process to come to a solution without your intervening. In fishing terms, you're giving professional leaders or students in your classroom one last chance to catch something on their own. The second, and the more important reason, is to see if someone in the group or the group as a collective whole can figure out which of the provided solutions is the correct answer without your intervention.

So if you are a professional leader reading this, or even if you are a student, and wondering if this idea has ever been used on you, the answer is probably yes. You just didn't know it. So the next time it is happening to you, pay attention to what is happening around you, recognize the situation for what it is, and stun the other professional leaders or the other students around you with your problem solving prowess. I promise you will be rewarded for this later.

Now it can certainly be argued that there are downsides to both letting the problem ripen and the baiting philosophy. However, if used in the appropriate situations, they can be wonderful opportunities to develop leadership capacity, to improve the collaborative process, to learn about the ability of other professional leaders or students to problem solve, and to gain an understanding about how other professional leaders or students respond under pressure in a difficult situation. All of this is knowledge to be used to your advantage and to be applied during the school change discussion and process either in your own classroom or with your entire staff.

As previously stated these are ideas to be used after a district has initiated the school change process, whatever the change may be. These are concepts to be used sparingly and carefully at the beginning of the school change process and more liberally and carefree during the implementation process and after the change has been clearly established. There is one other theory out there that may not be best practice in education, but can be helpful in promoting school change. But be aware, it may involve breaking things. . . .

CHAPTER 12

If It's Broke, Fix It with Duct Tape; If It's Not Broke, Break It, Then Fix It with Duct Tape

THE STORY

In 1997 Mr. Davis was an eighth-grade teacher in Wisconsin and had a bad habit of breaking things. His typical solution was to fix whatever it was that was broken with duct tape. As a result the teacher learned to always have a readily available supply of duct tape. One day, during study hall, the teacher dropped a stapler. Again. A student in his class had assumed that the teacher had broken it, so he said to the teacher, "Why don't you fix it with duct tape?" The teacher explained to the student that by some miracle it wasn't broken. "Then break it and fix it with duct tape." The teacher looked at the student in confusion. "Mr. Davis, I've been thinking a lot about this lately and I've come up with something for you to remember: 'If it's broke, fix it with duct tape. If it's not broke, break it, then fix it with duct tape.'" All Mr. Davis really could do at the time was laugh.

In his first year as a principal, Mr. Williams had a student come into his office from recess and asked him to come out to talk to the teacher on duty for recess. The teacher making this request was Mr. Davis. It was quite a hike from the office to the playground. "Why?" Mr. Williams asked the student. The student didn't know the answer, so Mr. Williams begrudgingly began the long trek out to the playground. When Mr. Williams got out to the playground, Mr. Davis was standing along the brick wall, very similar to the way a student might when they had gotten in trouble. "What can I do for you?" the principal asked.

Mr. Davis quickly explained what had happened. He was playing basketball with some students. When he bent over to pick up the basketball he split the entire crotch of his pants. Somehow, he had managed to back up to the wall and summon a student to go get Mr. Williams, all without being detected by any students. Mr. Davis turned around so Mr. Williams could see it while at the same time asking Mr. Williams how bad it was. That was probably the hardest Mr. Williams had laughed that school year. After recovering, Mr. Williams agreed to take over Mr. Davis's recess duty at that point so that he could go in and get it taken care of.

By "taken care of" Mr. Williams thought that Mr. Davis would change or go home to get a change of clothes, or any other solution that involved another pair of pants. So he was very surprised when he came in to see that Mr. Davis was still wearing the same pair of pants and an incredibly silly grin. Mr. Davis turned around again so Mr. Williams could see the back of his pants. Mr. Williams couldn't tell they had ever been split at all. "What happened?" he asked. You can guess what the response was. "Well, I learned something from a student the other day and I fixed my pants with duct tape," Mr. Davis stated proudly. And Mr. Davis taught the rest of the day in those pants and that silly grin. And somehow, some way, the students never knew.

THE THEORY

Whether you are an administrator or a teacher or a custodian, if you are a professional leader in education, you don't always have to believe in whatever the school change is that is being pitched. A professional leader just has to be able to sell it and convince others of the theory. If you have read the preceding story, you now know that it is possible that you can hide the split in your pants without the rest of the world knowing about it. Professional leaders can make something successful happen even if they don't believe in it. If you know it will improve student or teacher achievement and the district is asking you to participate, consider selling it through your actions regardless of whether you believe in it or not personally.

There is a quote from Albert Einstein that reads, "If the facts don't fit the theory, change the facts." If you as a professional leader are not comfortable with whatever school change is being pitched to you, keep in mind it is possible for you to change the facts of the school change being pitched so that it is a theory you and others around you can live with. Not agree with, but live with. And, again, if the change is something that you know is right for kids, you should consider being all for selling it even if you don't believe in it.

It is our responsibility at certain times to promote things we don't always agree with for the betterment of the district and to do what is best for kids. This can be the ultimate sacrifice for professional leaders in education. Compromising your own principles to do what is best for students is not always easy. It is easy to say we can do it because we are professionals, but another thing to follow through in our actions. But you know that you can do it and you should.

Many things in education are obviously broken and it is easy to be able to pick those things out. There are other things that may need to be broken and fixed or replaced altogether. Those things are the ones that are not as easily recognizable. Then there are those things that are not broken at all. If you don't go out of your way to break them, you may never realize that there is something better, maybe more efficient, maybe more cost effective, out there.

Regardless of whether you choose to fix or replace something that is broken or whether you choose to break something perfectly good to fix it, the *fix* is probably right under your nose, probably cheap and convenient. A recurring theme throughout this book is that the answer to whatever ails your district is right under your nose, it's free, and it's probably common sense. The same thing is being repeated again here. The *fix* is right there if you as a professional leader can master the ability to be open minded and objective enough to see it.

A question that gets asked all the time is: Why would you break something that is working just fine? It just doesn't make sense, they say. If it ain't broke, don't fix it. And it seems to go against my own commonsense beliefs. Well, maybe it does and maybe it doesn't. One of the most common ruts we get into in education is continuing to do the same things over and over again simply because that's the way it's always been done. Some will say that the definition of insanity is doing the same thing over and over again and expecting different results. Surely, whatever district you work in is not known for this, but trust me, they are out there. And in those districts they say things in one way or another that really means "Well, that's the way we've always done it."

That (whatever "that" is) is something that definitely needs to be purposely broken even though it may be working. Whatever "that" is, it is in the way of school change and progress and growth. However, if it is something that shows results in student achievement and is not in the way of progress, even if you've been doing it for fifty years, it is a good idea to leave that one alone. The real trick for all professional leaders is having or developing the ability to tell the difference between the two.

THE PRACTICE

What is true about the title of this chapter is that regardless of the problem existing or being created, you probably already have the solution at your disposal, sometimes without knowing it is there. Again you have read that over and over in the text here. Your solution probably is not duct tape to fix a split in the crotch of your pants, but it is something close to it, as weird as that sounds. As an administrator, your staff in essence is the duct tape. Use them as the solution. If you are a teacher, the duct tape solution may include the students in front of you or the other staff members around you. If you are a teacher you are also in the unique position of realizing that the solution might even be your administrator, as much as you may be uncomfortable in admitting that. For some of you, remember, they hired you, so they must be doing something right.

If you are paying attention even a little bit, you have picked up on the fact that it is critical that you create the culture you want first before you institute steps for change. This is no secret in the implementation of school change. If you can follow some simple commonsense steps, the type of personalities of your professional leaders will not matter so long as you have matched the right fit, done what you could to eliminate distractions, provided direction, and shown you love and care for those around you. After that, you have figured out when to let a problem ripen and when to break things to fix them, using duct tape as the fix of course.

Here is an example of how students can create the culture they want to institute steps for change. In talking with students about why they are not doing their homework, it is common that they will say (whether true or not) it is because they don't understand how to do the work. So I ask if they have asked the teacher for help. The students confirm that they have. How did you ask? I explain to students that if you just go up to a teacher after class to ask for help and say, "Hey, can you explain this to me again?" you have added to the problem. This always is received with a cross-eyed look.

So I explain further. When you ask that way a teacher will assume that the student is only asking because the student was not paying attention during the lesson. Isn't it possible that the student was paying attention, but he or she just doesn't get it? So I tell students to ask the teacher this way: Can you please explain this to me in another way? This subtle difference in questioning accomplishes two things. It tells a teacher that the student was paying attention during the lesson, but he or she just doesn't get it. And it forces the teacher to actually teach by finding another way to explain the same concept in a way that this particular student will understand. It is the duct tape solution. A simple thing that you can do to get what you want that is right under your nose.

If you have done those things first, the successful school change will come, whether that be in the classroom or district-wide. It can be done with a staff of very questioning and/or questionable professional leadership veterans that are about to retire, if you have the right fit and the right mindset. It can be done with an entire staff of rookies, if you have the right fit and the right mindset. The same is true if we are talking about students. Even the most hard core students will be with you if you have properly laid the same groundwork. Obviously in the professional leadership world, the dream situation is a mixture of both veterans and rookies working together for the good of the district and, more importantly, for what is best for kids in your district.

They say that there are certain horses that cannot be broken. They say that you cannot teach an old dog new tricks. For the sake of this argument, the rookie teachers are the horses and the veteran teachers are the old dogs. You are probably offended by this regardless of which category you have just been placed in, but follow me on this one. As we all know, education is a unique field. Perhaps the most unique field.

Because of that, you can throw those two ideas in the garbage because I do not agree that they apply to either the dog or the horse category. Because they are all professional leaders, when it comes to the horses and the old dogs in education, it is completely untrue that they cannot be broken or taught new tricks. In fact, sometimes it is only the horses and the old dogs that can be broken or taught new tricks.

Doesn't it seem silly that all this talk about school change and the use of common sense has brought us to the subjects of breaking things, the beauty of duct tape, old dogs, and horses? What a strange and beautiful profession we exist in when these things all have something in common. What an interesting culmination when there is a realization that these four things all have a related role to play in school change and the application of common sense in changing schools.

All of the limited knowledge relayed to you so far has dealt with what you would do, with what you could do, and with what you should do as it relates to school change and a common sense to the approach for successful school change. But to get where you want to go, you must first remember where you came from.

CHAPTER 13

Remembering Where You Came From

THE STORY

A little girl growing up in Texas had a wonderful childhood, all the right teachers, and all the right experiences. Very early on she had teachers that inspired and motivated her and she knew as a youngster that someday she wanted to be a teacher. As years went by, she continued to be a straight A student, went on to be a cheerleader for the high school football and basketball teams, had all the right friends and boyfriends and a family that loved and supported her.

Throughout those later years her vision of becoming a teacher began to get clearer and much more defined. She didn't just want to be a teacher, she wanted to be a third-grade teacher. She didn't just want to be a teacher anywhere, she wanted to be a teacher in Texas. And she didn't just want to be a teacher in Texas, she wanted to teach in her own hometown in the same grade school she went to. This was her dream and she never kept it a secret. In fact, she let the whole world know it.

She went on to the right college, married the right man, and had the right amount of children, who were intelligent and well behaved, by the way. She and her husband bought her parents' house, which was right across the street from the school where she grew up. Oh yes, and she became a third-grade teacher at the same grade school she went to, getting hired straight out of college after graduation.

During the infancy of her career she excelled in all areas of her teaching and she continues to do so today. She used to get teased by friends and colleagues not only for her dream but for never moving out of the town she grew up in. They gave her a hard time for never really getting out to see the world and spreading her wings. For becoming and living the story that sounded too good to be true.

These days she is respected and admired for the very same things she used to get teased for. It does sound too good to be true, doesn't it? But having the chance to live the dream happens all the time to people who remember where they came from and remember how they got there.

THE THEORY

Part of the struggle we all have as we get older, more settled, more secure, and more confident in our abilities is that we forget where we came from. How we got here. We want to resist change and all of the good things it can offer because we have gotten comfortable and change is not comfortable. It is not comfortable even when you have everything in place and have followed all of the rules and all of the directions. This comfort level that some of us enjoy so much in our personal and professional lives gets in the way of what we originally set out to accomplish in our careers. This can happen to professional leaders in education when we forget where we came from.

The story about the girl in Texas is a true story. What made her story unique is that her family did all the right things, her teachers did all the right things, and as a result, she did all the right things. That was her path to success and to following her dream. To this day, she always remembers where she came from and that is what motivated her to fulfill her own dreams.

She had a recognition very early on of how all of those people around her were playing a role in helping to set her up to be successful in whatever it was that she wanted to do. And because of that she was grateful, humbled, honored, and happy all at the same time. And she learned the most valuable lesson of all. She learned how and why it was important to pass that knowledge, those values, and those character traits on to the next generation.

The girl in the story understands what was needed in her world back then, what the next generation needs in their world now and in the future, and the significance of making sure there is a connection between those two worlds. That connection is so important because it isn't just about the values and the character traits that we all know serve as the connective tissue between knowledge and success. Using common sense in decision making and in our actions is also a part of that connective tissue. Whether that interpretation means a teacher teaching students in the classroom the importance of using common sense on the playground, or a superintendent using common sense in implementing school change in a school district is up to the reader. Either way, you get the idea.

All of this talk is similar to making the connection from today's educational world back to the days of the one-room schoolhouse. And now this girl from Texas is a champion for change in her school district. She grew up there; she knows the people, the climate, and the culture. And she knows what kind of change is best for her district, and let me tell you, it isn't always what research and best practice may tell you it should be. It isn't always going along with whatever the new trend in education happens to be. She uses common sense and the values of yesterday's educational world to figure that out.

People say that this generation of kids that we are dealing with now is much worse than any of the kids that have come before them. The same people say the next generation of kids will be even worse than that. The people who say these things do not know what they are talking about. Yes, kids today play more video games and spend way too much time on a computer or watching TV. Yes, they need more exercise and fresh air. Yes, they need to eat more home-cooked meals and less junk food. But the good kids are still just as polite and well mannered as they ever have been. The bad kids are no worse than they were a hundred years ago.

Society has changed and technology has advanced. But kids are still kids and that won't ever change. You might be forgetting that because you have gotten too comfortable. The people who say those things certainly have gotten way too comfortable. But if we remember where we came from and how we got here, not only does it refocus and re-energize our thoughts about students, it refocuses our thoughts about everything. It makes us realize why we got into the game of education. It makes us realize why change in education is good and beautiful even when it is uncomfortable and awkward.

CHAPTER 13

THE PRACTICE

So the story of the good girl making it good is nice. I'll bet you were waiting for a terrible ending. Or perhaps you were wondering why the chapter didn't start with a hard luck story that had a happy ending. That is what everyone does. Remember, these stories are real. Besides, there is one of those hard luck kinds of stories in chapter 14. Anyway, there is a practice behind this theory, believe it or not.

There are things we can do to remember where we came from when we get in a rut. To remember how we got here. There are things to think about when we get too comfortable, either personally or professionally, or both. We fall back to what we know; we think about our own past.

So where did you come from? Was it somewhere good like the girl from Texas or was it someplace that you only think about so you realize how good you have it now? How exactly did you get here? Did you take the easy road where your parents paid for your car, your insurance, or your college? Did you take the hard road, scratching and clawing every step of the way just for the smallest edge? Guess what, one isn't better than the other; the point is, how did you get here? Are you having trouble remembering? Don't want to remember? It might be because you've gotten too comfortable.

Let me help you. Remember when you were a kid and your mom opened the door for you so you could carry your toys out to the yard? That's why you used to hold the door open for students entering your classroom when you first started teaching. That's why you held the door open for other professional leaders coming to a staff meeting when you first became principal.

Remember when you were in junior high and you had to move because your dad got a new job? You were traumatized and thought you would never be able to go on. Some time went by and all of the teachers at the new school went out of their way to help you get adjusted. They got you involved and made sure other kids showed you the ropes. That move became the single most life-changing event that made you want to become a professional leader in education. It is the reason why you used to help the new kids in your district get acclimated and why you used to go out of your way to make sure they were watched over.

Opening the door, helping others get acclimated, that's where you came from. Wanting to do the right thing and changing the world in your own little way, that's where you came from. Wanting to make a difference in the lives of others, that's where you came from. Believing in the American Dream and believing you can help others reach their dreams too, that's where you came from.

Now, do you remember how you got here? No? Remember when you were in high school and you stayed up all night to finish an assignment, not just for a good grade, but to impress someone? That's why you used to remind your students and your colleagues that procrastination is a bad habit. That's why you used to remind your students and your colleagues that it is okay to go above and beyond the requirements once in a while. And that's how you got here.

Remember when you were in college and you drove four hours with five of your best friends because you absolutely had to see your favorite band in concert that night? That's why you used to recognize the importance of music in a child's life even though you couldn't play an instrument to save your life. That is why you used to recognize that there is a student in your class that would fail every academic class if they were not in band, so you got them to sign up when their parents would not sign the form. That's why you used to love to take your class to music. Not because you were looking forward to the prep time that you'd spend doing no prep, but because you knew the importance of music in a child's development. That's how you got here.

Remember when you were in high school and a teacher told you that you'd never amount to anything? You were so irritated that you spent the rest of your academic career trying to prove them wrong? Well, guess what? Now you have. It is for this reason that you used to help the students that you knew might not make it. Proving everyone wrong, that's where you came from and how you got here.

Regardless of where you came from or how you got here, it is important that you remember. No story is better than another, whether it was a Cinderella one or a silver spoon one. Whatever your path was, if you remember it, it makes you stronger and more appreciative of what you have. It makes you realize your role as a professional leader in successful school change. And that is to provide the same opportunity, the same path, for other professional leaders, for students, for your school district.

There is one final story that might help you to realize all of the things that you have already done for students and for your district, and that you may not yet realize that you have done. And this final story might serve as a last reminder as to why you got into this game to begin with and why your own district cannot, I said *cannot*, achieve successful, sustained school change in your district without you.

CHAPTER 14

The Final Story

In small towns, and probably large cities as well, all across the country sports live and breathe fire and life into the culture of the community and the school environment. It is something that is near and dear to people's hearts, sometimes for good reason. Sports are, for a very small minority of students, the only way out. For other students who may not be straight A students, art can be a way out. Music can be a way out. Cooking can be a way out. And on and on. But for a lot of people in and out of education, by sheer popularity, sports seem to be the inaccurate focus as a way out.

This is true even though it is widely acknowledged that for a majority of the student population, education should really be the only real way out. However, as a result of sports being more popular, it is easy for students and athletes and citizens alike to get caught up in the novelty of it all, especially when the sporting priority is encouraged by parents and citizens of the community.

A long time ago, in a small community in Wisconsin, a boy got caught up in sports like so many others before him. But there is a uniqueness to his story that is different from others. What is unique is that his story ends differently. At his high school in central Wisconsin back then, a student could get all Ds and two Fs and still be eligible. So for the first three years in high school he got all Ds and two Fs and focused on playing sports.

The son of a farmer and a homemaker, he was a hard worker who had worked on farms and had been driving a tractor since he was eight. Believe it or not, for those of you in the real world, yes, this type of stuff, even in our advanced technological society, still does happen in today's world. This student was an average athlete at best, but was very artistic. And he was a senior in high school before he realized it might be a good idea to put forth some effort in school in something besides sports. When he finally did as senior, he got straight As. His art teacher pulled him aside during class one day. She said to him, "If I fill out some applications for college for you, will you do the rest of the work if anything comes of it?" Thinking his art teacher was off her rocker and was joking with him, he laughed as he replied, "Sure thing."

He never thought about it again and as the school year was winding down, he was certain he would spend his life working one of the large mint farms in the area, as he had done for the past two summers. And, strangely enough, he was blissful in the reality of doing so. But late in the spring he received a letter from the only college his art teacher had applied to for him. As he had a cumulative high school GPA of 2.0, the college was very hesitant in their approach. The college had sent a letter that requested three letters of recommendation from his high school teachers just to be able to consider him. With his tail between his legs, he begged three of the teachers whose classes he had been screwing around in for the past three years to write him a letter. Somehow, some way, he got three teachers to agree and he sent them in. Again, he never thought another thing about it.

After graduation and another long but satisfying summer working on the mint farm, late in August he received another letter from the college stating that he had been accepted on probation. The letter stated that any grade lower than a C in the first semester would send him back home. He did not know where the college was and had never even visited the campus. But at the end of August, he packed up his 1972 green and rusting AMC Hornet and began the drive.

The trip that should have taken a couple of hours ended up taking five hours because he could not find the school. Though the address was in Milwaukee, it was actually located in a very well-to-do northern suburb, just across the street from the richest public school district in the state of Wisconsin. When he finally pulled into the lot, he parked among other students' brand new BMWs, Porsches, and Corvettes.

There were upperclassmen there to help the new students move in. Though this was not standard procedure at colleges back then, it was a very nice touch. But no one came to help him. He wanted to drive back home, but remembered his promise to his old art teacher. Embarrassed and feeling like a beaten dog with his tail still between his legs, he began to move his things in by himself.

That first semester he had to learn how to learn. That's right, he had to learn how to learn. The learning curve was brutal. As other students spent their time getting to know each other, going to parties on the weekends, and going to social gatherings all over the campus throughout the week, he never left his room. And just to be able to survive, he learned how to learn.

I'm sure it comes as no surprise that in that first semester he barely made it. However, every semester after that, he was on the Dean's List, eventually changing his focus to becoming a teacher, of all things. He also made friends over time and learned to fit in with other students, even though most of them came from drastically different backgrounds. However, by the time he graduated, the other students, friends or not, never knew where he came from or how he got there. Here's the success part. He graduated and got a job teaching in a public school district early that summer.

Later in the summer, when in his classroom working and preparing for his upcoming first year of teaching, another teacher from across the hall came in and introduced herself. "What grade are you in?" she asked. Thinking the other teacher was asking him what grade he was teaching, he replied, "Sixth grade." "You look kind of old to be a sixth grader." And thus, he was indoctrinated into the world of education and its sometimes weird little quirks. This was his very first inclination that professional leaders in the field of education sometimes make the mistake of equating experience with competence or quality.

If you are a professional leader looking to implement change, follow the advice given here to lay the proper groundwork and to include veteran professional leaders carefully. Obviously, they are always the key to successful school change. However, also be very mindful of newer teachers in your district. Tap into that resource like you may have never done before. The reason why this is critical is because it is this group that will lead the district into the future. They alone may have the "now" generational skills to do so. Even the veteran professional leaders in your district will give you the same advice if they see the bigger picture and are being honest about what it is that they see. And don't make the foolish mistake of thinking that they are not as equally qualified to help implement school change (though they may not be if you did not follow the advice given in chapters 3 and 4) as the most veteran professional leader on your staff.

Okay, back to the story. You want to know what happened, right? One year later, after being hired as a sixth-grade teacher, he was interviewing for a teaching job at another public school district nearby. The reason why might be answered in a different book. Anyway, the principal asked him the following question: "Where do you see yourself personally and professionally ten years from now?" "Sitting in your chair asking potential teaching candidates that same question" was his response. And yes, ten years later, almost to the day, he was the principal at that school interviewing teacher candidates. It sounds familiar, right? That's because this is the same kid that was talked about in the story beginning chapter 3.

THE THEORY

You never know where success may come from. Even as well as you may know your students, your staff, your colleagues, sometimes you still never really know where they came from. You never know where inspiration for them might come from. Sometimes it may come to you from the most unlikely of sources. Sometimes you have to go out and find it on your own. But if you've been a professional leader for some time now, this is no surprise to you.

A former student of mine is a self-taught musician that is an incredible talent. As an eighth-grade student he was shy and humble and bright. As an adult now he is the same, at least when he is off the stage and out of the bright lights. He was a terrible athlete back then, but willing to run through the wall if you asked him to. He made the basketball team on that fact alone. But he didn't always quite fit in and he knew it and I knew it. He seemed to always be trying to find his place and where he fit in.

When he graduated high school, he was so interested in music and singing that he did not go to college, though he certainly could have.

Instead, he wanted to pursue his musical interests, and thankfully he did, even against my own advice to him. After a couple of years wallowing around with a mediocre band, some deadbeat friends, bad experiences with women, and a dead-end job, he took a chance. Not known for taking chances, he had done the right thing this time.

You see, he traded in his car for a van, packed all of his stuff, and took the little money he had and drove to Los Angeles. He got a couple of gigs, got noticed, and all of the sudden he's in a recording studio and touring. Like I said, the guy is an unbelievable talent. He's going to be big someday, and in my mind he already is. But even if he is not, he's already reached his dreams. The point is, it can happen to you, and if you are a professional leader it already has. It can happen to your students. You can help to make it happen for your students. You can make change happen for your district. It happens every day. Sometimes it just takes a professional leader who recognizes, a little bit of reaching out, and stepping out of your comfort zone or taking a chance just once in a while.

Education in its truest form and a part of the American Dream is based on the premise of taking a chance once in a while. Maybe stepping out of your comfort zone once in a while. Sometimes it is a calculated risk. This former student of mine is doing his thing and living his own part of the American Dream. Congratulations to him for finding his place in the world. And to all of our former students that have gone on to do something wonderful, whether that is making music or flipping burgers if that's your thing, congratulations to you as well. They are well deserving of our congratulations because whether they are now famous or totally inconspicuous, as a result of our guidance and professionalism, we have somehow played a small part in their success. And whether you realize it or not, we are pumping out successful, functioning citizens every day. They may not be famous, but they are successful in society so long as they are doing right by themselves and by what we have taught them. We are in the only professional field on the planet that can claim that as a reality.

So what do these former students have to do with successful school change? Their stories are lessons to us all that the commonsense values that we have taught them have paid off. That the ideals that we were so careful to teach and that have been properly taught have indeed stood the test of time. That the one-room schoolhouse ideals so important back then are still important today, as convoluted as they may have become in our eagerness to advance. Theirs are lessons that we can learn from now.

Theirs are lessons that teach us to be sure to pay the same amount of attention to all students and to all professional leaders. If you are an administrator you probably have the next greatest teacher right before your eyes and neither you nor they know it yet. If you are a teacher, whether you realize it or not, the students before you are not just regular, run-of-the-mill students. Someone before you, and sometimes a whole group, will be great. Neither you nor they know it yet. And whether it is you as an administrator or you as a teacher, there is a certainty that the great students before you need you to bring it out of them. To help them make their dreams come true.

Let's reiterate for effect. Take a good, long, hard look. If you are an administrator and you have followed some sound commonsense practice, the professional leaders you should see before you all have the ability to be great. It is they that are the champions of school change, not the administrators or the school boards. They are needing and actually wanting you to help them get it out of them.

If you are a teacher, the students you should now see before you are the next generation of doctors, lawyers, and yes, maybe teachers. They are also the ones who will be flipping your burgers or steaks at the restaurant you like so much. Heck, they might be the owners. They are the politicians that might irritate you to no end and yet they may also be the musicians and the thespians that will relieve the stress you feel daily. They are the ones who will build our roads and our houses and advance our technology, including building our computers. They are the police officers and military personnel that will keep you and your children and your grandchildren safe. And here's something that should really make you step back and rethink how you interact with your students: the students before you right now are the people who will take care of you one day when you are older and when no one else will. So now think about that one for effect.

Despite what some experts may tell you, there is no standard or secret formula to accomplishing successful change in schools. I would love to lie and say, hey, follow this expert or that professional leader.

And without a doubt, there are certainly some tips here that are helpful as well. But in the end, common sense should tell you that despite what best practices dictate and what experts say and write, there is another thing to consider in introducing successful change to your district. Professional leaders should take best practices into consideration, but ultimately, a really good professional leader does what is best for their individual district or school. This may mean taking everything experts and best practices tell you and certainly considering it, but maybe also throwing it out the window. This may mean following everything experts and best practices tell you to do to the letter, but it may also mean telling them to shove it.

Professional leaders should *always* do what is best for their district. Always. Believe it or not, this may also mean not following best practice. Get used to that idea because it may be a reality for you, depending on the district you work in. Again, best practice does not always mean best for your district, contrary to public belief. This idea, combined with the knowledge that all teachers and all students have the potential to be great, is what should guide leadership and successful school change. Period.

It's a matter of staying on the side of the kids and the faculty, no matter who pressures you to do otherwise. It can be risky and it can sometimes be lonely to do so because the kids and the faculty do not have the power or the money or the political pull that other interests do. But in most cases, if you take the side of the kids and the faculty, then you are doing the correct moral thing.

A teacher once said to me, "Well, you know, summer school will never help Johnny anyway. It's not like he's ever going to be ready for the next school year anyway." Rarely have I ever been more irritated at another professional leader. I tried to explain in vain to that teacher that it is the Johnnies that are running the world right now. That, my friends, is the reality of our world today. The popular kids aren't running the world anymore and neither are the straight A students that went to the right university. Too many things, including technology and the Internet, have leveled the playing field, intelligence notwithstanding. But I could tell it was not registering with this teacher. So I asked the teacher this question: "If you do not believe in Johnny, who ever will?"

Never underestimate the power of one teacher, the power of one student. Never underestimate the ability of those before you. Tap into it first, then make whatever judgment you deem necessary. Never forget that the professional leader or the student you may think is the lowest of the group or the most misbehaved has dreams also. It is they that are the ones that have the most to teach professional leaders in education about following dreams. And it is they that may have or be the answer you have been looking for, if only you could be objective enough to see it. You may be the answer they have been looking for. But if we cannot find a way to reach them, who will? If they cannot find a way to connect with you, how can they succeed? If we cannot find a way to believe in them, who will?

THE PRACTICE

Ahh, there's so many gems. Polishing the sparkly ones is the easy part. The trouble is in finding the nastiest, most scratched-up piece of coal and making it shine, too. How do we tell which professional leader or which student is the next greatest thing? This, too, can be simple. Just look. Not just at the likely sources, the brilliant diamonds, but more importantly, at the unlikely sources, the coal. Most times all it takes is the application of the senses. If you can objectively look, listen, and feel, common sense and instinct will prevail and it will come to you.

You have been in education long enough now that you are a trained machine. You just don't know it. Get back to your roots; remember the game you came to play. The longer you are in education, if you are the true professional you claim to be, you look for the challenge of the next professional leader, the next student, the next class. Instead of getting comfortable in your tenure, you look for the next thing that will heighten your senses. I challenge you right now to begin doing that again with the beginning of every new school year. I challenge you to look for things to heighten your senses until the day you retire. You owe that to yourself, to your district, and most importantly, to the students in front of you.

In mentioning unlikely sources remember also that if you are an administrator looking for another professional leader to help with promoting school change, then look first to the veterans, not to the whippersnappers. The education field is one of a very few in which you can teach an old dog new tricks. Some of those old dogs are not only wanting to learn a new trick, but are eager to learn one sometimes just for the sake of their own sanity and professional development.

Starting with the veterans, not ending with them, is a great idea that we all know is not foolproof. It could make the change process much easier. Frequently, however, the veterans are overlooked. I don't understand when this still happens because it is commonly known as a big mistake and one that could work against you later. This same idea could hold true for teachers wanting to try something new in their classrooms. It may actually make some sense to try it out first with the kids who have already been around the block a few times.

Work with a drive and an action that has purposeful meaning to it. Don't be afraid to have a passion and let it shine through now and then. Gary Vaynerchuk would love you if you did. Who is Gary Vaynerchuk? He is one of those rare individuals who speaks and who writes in a way that transcends all fields. Gary's message can be applied in many ways in our field, even though he probably knows little about education. I highly recommend his book *Crush It!* (2009).

Gary's book will prioritize you, focus you, energize you, and will show you why it is important to let your passion shine through once in a while. He will also tell you that by doing so, those around you will know you care. When other professional leaders or your students know you care, it becomes much easier to forgive mistakes made in action or in words throughout the change process. It allows the process to continue on undamaged and without stopping to have to make repairs.

So how do you believe? How do you find a way to reach the professional leader or the student that cannot be reached? If common sense ever applied to a situation, this is it right here. The answer is so simple and the younger the professional leader or the student is, the easier the solution becomes. Find out what makes them tick. It is easier the younger the student is because they have not yet learned how to hide what makes them tick. Regardless, the challenge is clear.

Conclusion: You've Got to Keep Them Separated

Let's remember how we started. Successful school change can happen for districts that have been failing. But making sure that success is sustained over time is the bigger issue. Whether you work in a school or a district that has experienced success or not, the first step is knowing in advance how to avoid the traps of success once you get there. Knowing that one thing first, ahead of anything else, sets the tone that you as a professional leader are expecting to achieve success, either as an individual or as a district or both. This is the first step to getting yourself and others moving in the right direction. Expect success and nothing less.

Once you know this, it allows you to proceed with everything else that can follow. School change begins first with the right state of mind. Worrying about things that are unfair only impedes the process. Set the groundwork by reminding professional leaders why they got into the game. No more worrying about things you cannot control. No more worrying about perceptions about what may or may not be fair. True professionals are concerned with taking care of their own students first and letting everything else take care of itself. And they all already know this, but might need to be and maybe even want to be reminded of it from time to time.

You have begun the groundwork for changing expectations and how we think about success and change in schools. Get the right fit. This is maybe the most difficult thing to do because of the ugliness that is sometimes involved. As written about in chapter 3, this could potentially involve a kitchen cleaning process, difficult decisions about tenure, and a revamping of your hiring process. Do this correctly and with some common sense and a lot of other things discussed in chapters 4 through 12 will fall nicely in line.

The commonsense approach should start at the top. Yes, I am talking about school boards. This will be the only time in this book that I talk politics, because I also can't stand them. Thank goodness it is during the conclusion. Something must be done about the process of how we elect school board members. Until that happens, some school districts will always be in trouble.

A lot of my colleagues explain it like this. Imagine one day in the business world that a Fortune 500 company picked five or seven people randomly off of the street to run the company. How long would the company be able to survive, given the likely lack of business knowledge of the five to seven random people picked off of the streets? There are states where there are very limited requirements to run for the school board. In some states you just have to be a citizen who is eighteen years old. As a result, there are schools in the country that are being run by people who do not know the first thing about the educational process. It seems silly that this process could be a productive or a positive thing. Despite the conflict of interest that may arise, it also seems silly that professional leaders sometimes have literally no input into who will ultimately run the school. Yes, they should definitely be elected positions, but how can certain school districts possibly implement successful school change under these conditions?

Having said that, there are very good school districts that have figured it out. They have groomed their current board members into selecting their successors based on solid educational reasons. They have also found other legitimate ways to beat the system in getting the right people on the board. There will be no advice given on that subject here. However, the intent is to give just the slightest indication to professional leaders that if you look hard enough, you too can find the ways around, and like many other educational solutions, they are probably right under your nose and cost nothing.

Professional leaders, be fair to all who come before you. Teacher leaders, be fair to all of your students. You never know when they may have to be your biggest supporters. In education sometimes it is difficult to separate. It is hard to not let one thing affect another unnecessarily. Sometimes we do it subconsciously without ever realizing it. For example, students in trouble often would come into the principal's office explaining that they did something bad because of something that happened away from school. And the principal must explain the importance of keeping them separated.

In the story that follows, a principal puts a student in the seat where the principal sits in order to clarify why it is important to "keep them separated." The principal explains that earlier in the day a different student came into the office that made the principal really upset. The principal asks the student sitting before her now if it would be fair of the principal to start yelling at this student, when she didn't even know what the student did yet, because she was still mad at the other student that had come into the office earlier in the day. This student, of course, will always say no. The principal then asks the student if it is okay for the principal to get into an argument with her spouse when she gets home because she was upset about the kids who had come into the office that day or because she did not agree with her boss at school. Again the student would say no.

At one time in my principal life, I applied a different "keep them separated" explanation to a student. There are fifty teachers that work for me at the school and I asked the student if he thought I liked every one of them. The student thinks about it and correctly answers "no." I then asked the student if it is okay for me to treat the teachers that I don't like differently just because I don't like them. And the further I go on with this, the clearer the message becomes to the student and it really begins to sink in. That or else the student was just pretending it sank in so they didn't have to hear the lecture anymore. Either way, it is a happy ending and the point is made. You have to keep them separated.

It would be wise of many districts to take this same approach with the professional leaders under their care. The very good districts have a concern about the mental, social, and physical well-being of all of the professional leaders who work for them during and after their careers. They make it known what the district priorities outside of education really are. They make it known that while it is clearly healthy to reflect on your profession on a daily basis, it should not interfere with the enjoyment of your time spent away from your profession. Family is first, religion is second, a lot of other things are third, and your job in education is fourth. Even though your job in education is the most important one in the world today, it is not your first priority. It is your fourth.

The really good districts make sure their employees know the difference between what is healthy and what is obsessive. What is healthy is taking a few minutes at the end of each day to think about what ways you could improve as a professional leader and how you could have done things differently that day. Reflection is a healthy and necessary element to the profession, though it can be argued that spending more than a few minutes a day is obsessive and may not be healthy or productive. Spending hours on end past your contracted time at school does not make you a better administrator, a better teacher, or a better professional leader. It is the quality of the time that you work that matters and spending that much time at your profession is a sign of the inability to keep them separated.

They say to work smarter, not harder. If you are a professional leader that has a family but you spend no time mastering this skill, then what you need is a serious priority evaluation. Live the example that you expect from your students and from other professional leaders around you. Working smarter is a requirement for sanity but also for successful school change. Working harder guarantees absolutely nothing if you think the definition of working harder is working longer hours simply to say you are working harder.

All of us have heard another phrase, "Common sense isn't always common," and it begs the question, Why isn't it always common? I wish I knew the answer and that I could write about it right here. But I do not. What I can tell you with great certainty is that professional leaders follow certain guidelines in making important decisions about school leadership and change: study the data, research best practices, have a sound argument, have a sound plan.

Sounds great in theory, right? Yet something is missing. At the end of the day and most certainly in any time of uncertainty, trust your own ability and in the ability of those around you. Trust your own gut instinct and do what is in the best interest of your own school and your own district. Do this regardless of what the new trends are and regardless of what the experts tell you. Professional leaders who are confident in their own abilities and trust in the abilities of those around them are the ones who will initiate the notion that getting change in schools "back to common sense" be a commonplace instead of a rarity.

For those that have read this book, I truly hope that it has accomplished two things to some small degree. The first is that I hope you had a "duh" moment for every point made. A "you already knew that, you just needed to be reminded" kind of a thing. Almost like a feeling that by the end you felt like maybe you didn't really need to read to the book at all because it is all common sense.

The second thing is much more important and it is to reflect on some questions. Do you remember why you got into this game? Was it because you wanted to change the world? Was it because you wanted to make a difference? Was it because you wanted to experience the pure joy of bettering a child's life through education? You better damn well believe it. Over time we can lose focus because we are never reminded of it on a continuous basis over the span of our careers.

I will tell you this. Even the worst teachers in your school have either past or present student fans, or both, somewhere that think they are the greatest. It's just that no one knows it. Last year there was a student that went home crying on the last day of school because he or she would not have you for a teacher next year. And yes, that could be a second grader or a junior in high school. When this school year began, there were a couple of students that could not focus in their classroom. It's because they were instead wondering what you were doing in your classroom. Even if you are the most boring teacher in the world, somewhere there is a student, or a former student, or both, dying to get to your class just to see or hear what you are going to do next.

There's a whole horde of former graduates that attribute to you everything they've accomplished in their postgraduate lives, whether they are flipping burgers at McDonald's or performing surgery on the president. Why don't you know this? How could you have missed this? Because it is human nature to avoid both confrontation and praise equally. Which means here is your answer: it is a very rare day indeed that students, past or present, are ever going to actually tell you that you are responsible for their success. Or that you were the inspiration that helped them to change the world, to make a difference in their own little way. And on a side note, just so you are aware if you weren't already, that type of change and difference can happen both in the drive-through and in the operating room.

So why haven't they already told you? Because it is too inconvenient. It is just like telling people something they don't want to hear; it's too uncomfortable. They have their own lives now. Rest assured, however, they have already told their spouses, their kids, their friends, and their colleagues. And when you really think about it, it does make sense. Who is the one teacher that ever really motivated and inspired you? Does he or she know it? Have you ever told him or her? Though you've probably told countless other people close to you, have you ever really told him or her? For most of us, I doubt it.

A mark of maturity for teachers is letting go. Most of teaching should be letting go and being happy that former students don't come around you anymore. That is usually a sign that things are right with the world. Students shouldn't be coming back to see you all of the time if you have done a great job with them.

So guess what's been happening all this time that you thought you were just wallowing about and that no one cares? So what's been going on all these years you've never known if you were reaching them, if anyone even noticed? You've been changing the world, that's what. One student at a time. You've been making a difference doing the most important job in the entire world. Whether you teach in kindergarten or are the superintendent at a high school, you've changed the life of a child on a daily basis and made the world a better place in your own little way. You just don't know it.

Now is the time again to be a true professional leader. Lead the change or follow those who are leading the change, whichever suits your nature and your personality. Either way, get back in the game. One isn't better than the other, but the district you work in cannot achieve or sustain successful school change without you. Remember why you got into this game? Now get back in the game again. It's time and it's common sense.

Some say that the days of the American Dream are gone. The days of following your dreams and being able to achieve them are gone. What a crock. Not only is that not true, but I would argue that the American Dream is just about to catch its second wind. The advance of the Internet, and technology in general, have leveled the playing field more than any other thing in our history. Our profession is about to have the opportunity to strike while the iron is hot, which would allow more of our students and our own children and grandchildren to achieve the American Dream than ever before.

But it will only happen if we change how we think about embracing change and success in schools in general. There are times when you should forget about test scores and apply common sense. We've been able to survive up to this point because of our ability to be able to adapt, both in and out of education. However, in education, we are reaching a fork in the road because of the rate at which we've been adapting to change and the outside world around us. Because of all of the advances, it is soon going to be necessary that we as professional leaders in education are not only more fully embracing of change, but that we embrace it and achieve school change at a much faster pace than we've ever been used to before if we want to keep the American Dream alive for all that follow us. And it can be done. It can be so easy.

They say that education isn't what it used to be. The curriculum is watered down, test scores have gone down, we've fallen behind other countries, we're doing the same things we have for years and years. And with some of that they might be right, I hate to say. But remember, we as professional leaders in education have little control over things like where priorities are placed, societal changes, where money is spent, what curriculum is taught, and so on. Even though at times we like to think we do, we really do not.

And as for doing things the same way for years, that is certainly an issue. However, there is one good thing that has been used going all the way back to the days of the one-room schoolhouse. It is something that I believe should be used even more and be more of a focus when we talk about how to embrace school change and how to achieve school change. And even in today's ever-changing world and with all of the advances we've made since the days of the one-room schoolhouse, it still applies now, maybe more than ever. It's called common sense.

A book would not be complete without thanks. Priorities, priorities. Special thanks to all of my family and friends, but especially to my wonderful wife, Ruth, and our two boys. My family and friends have to put up with me once in a while, but Ruth has had to put up with me every day since we met. Once you get to know me, you'll understand the magnitude of that endeavor. Thanks to all of my colleagues, both past and present. This includes support staff, teachers, administrators, various school board members, and countless other professional leaders in and out of education.

Thanks to all of my undergraduate instructors at Cardinal Stritch University who helped me realize my calling and turned me not only into an actual real, functioning person but a professional educator. A thank you also has to be given to all of my graduate professors at Aurora University, but specifically to those at the beautiful George Williams campus in Williams Bay, Wisconsin. Even more specifically to Dr. Jim Sorenson, a motivator and an inspiration to me without ever knowing it, which are truly the best kinds. As intelligent as he may be, no one applies more common sense and logic to situations than he does. It was a discussion during one of his graduate courses that was the inspiration behind chapter 11. And to Dr. Faith Wilson, possibly the most brilliant person I've come across. Serving as an editor and a source of inspiration, she has played a critical role in opening my mind and my eyes to new worlds I had not previously known or seen. She has accomplished this for me and for so many others simply by sharing her own world views and modeling how to really listen. Sorry, Dr. Wilson, for not having more research and more references, maybe the next book.

Thank you to Nick Kysely and www.brookstonestudios.com for helping with the cover. A special thank you to former student Mike McCarville, who is a teacher now, but many years back gave me the inspiration and the title for chapter 12. A thank you also to Kevin Hammond and countless other former students that have recently reminded me not only of why I got into the game, but of the reality that not only is it still possible to follow your dreams, it is more possible now than ever before. A thank you to my brother-in-law, one of my all-time heroes, and to every other member of the military and their families, past and present, for allowing me to be able to freely write what I want to here. Finally, and perhaps it could be argued most importantly, to everyone at Rowman & Littlefield, including Maera Stratton and Elaine McGarraugh. And more specifically to Tom Koerner, who took a chance on me when no one else would. Story of my life, but that also is for a different book. Anyway, thanks again, Tom. I leave you with this . . .

> Who the Author of this Publication is, is wholly unnecessary to the public, as the object for attention is the Doctrine Itself, not the man. Yet it may not be unnecessary to say, that he is unconnected with any Party, and under no sort of influence public or private, but the influence of reason and principle. —Thomas Paine, *Common Sense*, 1776

References

Bolman, L. G., and Deal, T. E. (1997). *Reframing Organizations*. San Francisco: Jossey-Bass.

Curl, A. L., and Townsend, A. L. (2008). "Retirement Transitions among Married Couples." http://jwbh.haworthpress.com.

Fullan, M. (2008). *The Six Secrets of Change*. San Francisco: Jossey-Bass.

Johnson, D. (2005). *Sustaining Change in Schools*. Alexandria, VA: Association for Supervision and Curriculum Development.

Paine, T. (1776). *Common Sense*.

Pollock, J. (2007). *Improving Student Learning One Teacher at a Time*. Alexandria, VA: Association for Supervision and Curriculum Development.

Reeves, D.B. (2009). *Leading Change in Your School*. Alexandria, VA: Association for Supervision and Curriculum Development.

Sergiovanni, T. J., and Starratt, R. J. (2002). *Supervision: A Redefinition*. New York: McGraw-Hill.

Sternberg, R. (2004). "Filling the Voids in Retirement: Your Emotions and Finances." *School Administrator* 36.

Vaynerchuk, G. (2009). *Crush It! Why Now Is the Time to Cash in on Your Passion*. New York: HarperCollins.

About the Author

After graduating with a bachelor's degree from Cardinal Stritch College (now Cardinal Stritch University), **Joe Dawidziak** began his professional teaching career as a sixth-grade teacher in 1995, later becoming an eighth-grade teacher for eight years. After receiving a master's degree in educational leadership, Joe began his career in educational administration as a principal, a position he currently holds.

A fan of the underdog, his own story is one of beating the odds. After being told he would never amount to anything by his teachers in high school and being told that he wasn't good enough at the graduate level, Joe is currently working on his Ph.D. and has already accomplished many of his own dreams. He is a believer that it can happen for you too, regardless of age, race, economic status, or any other label. Joe currently resides with his wife and two boys in Burlington, Wisconsin, and can be reached at joedawidziak@gmail.com.

www.ingramcontent.com/pod-product-compliance
Lightning Source LLC
Chambersburg PA
CBHW022015300426
44117CB00005B/209